God's Magnificent Creatures

Lessons Learned From God's Backyard Creatures

Mary Rogers

Copyright © April 30, 2025, by Mary Rogers

All rights reserved. No part of this book may be reproduced or used in any manner without written permission of the copyright owner except for the use of quotations in a book review.

Front cover design by:

www.SelfPubBookCovers.com/RLSather

Published by:

Legacy Lane Publishing

Weatherford, TX

ISBN:978-1-954800-27-4

THANK YOU

God – Thank you for your grace, mercy, unconditional love, gift of salvation and the many principles and promises in the Bible that have encouraged me to grow as a Christian in a fallen world. Thank you for the gifts you have given me to further my walk for your kingdom.

Mark Rogers – My husband of 38 years. I don't believe I would have ever noticed or enjoyed nature and its many creatures if I had not met and married you. Your child like enthusiasm for hunting and fishing at times is contagious. Thank you for tolerating me during this process. There were many times when my frustration and lack of technology knowledge threw me into a personality change. Thank you for being patient and my tech person at times. I love you!

Mary Rodman (the other Aunt Mary) – You are an answered prayer! I am not a technology person and have always struggled with understanding how to use computers, etc. My prayer was, God, if you want me to write and publish this book, you will have to put people in my life who can help me with all of this technology. And here you came! You have been a blessing and a help beyond what words can say. Your gift of wanting to help people and your patience and your strong faith, shows God's love. Thank you for the tireless hours and many phone calls you put into my project to make this a dream come true. Thank you, my friend!

Cheryll Jude – You are another answered prayer! Thank you for sacrificing your time to scan my stories into my new laptop. You were the catalyst that got things moving forward. Your gift of encouragement has not only been a blessing to me but others as well. I like to surround myself with people who feel like sunshine and you are one of them. Thank you, my friend!

Aaron Riddle – You are also an answered prayer! God does answer prayer! Your computer skills amaze me. God has given you such talent to help others in this ever-growing tech world. Thank you for your patience and for giving up family time to share your gifts!

Evelyn Grissom – Grammer and talking was never my forte! Thank you for your proofreading skills and for leaving some of the real me in the stories. Your growing family is a testimony of God's obedience. So proud of the mother and grandmother you have become. I am grateful you are my sister!

Jeanette Kassebaum – Thank you for your suggestions, biography help, zoom meeting, and listening in my times of frustration when I thought the adversary was winning during this process. I have always looked up to you and your ambition to have your own law practice that is run with such integrity. You have always been an inspiration to me! I am grateful you are my sister!

Deb Oakley & Delores Teal – Thank you both for your words of encouragement over the phone. Moving away has brought its friendship challenges and I am so grateful we are still able to stay in touch, even if it's only by phone. Delores, thank you for the sparkly turtle. It sits on my desk reminding me that sometimes projects in life move slower than we expect. It's all in Gods timing! Thank you, my friends!

Contents

THE BAT HOUSE	1
EXPECTATIONS	19
LITTLE CHURCH MOUSE	27
LIGHT VERSUS DARK	33
SONG IN OUR HEARTS	37
FEAR	41
THE COMFORTER	49
UNITY	53
INSTINCT	59
OBADIAH	67
PERSEVERANCE	73
LET YOUR LIGHT SHINE	79
FOUNDATION	83
PURPOSE	87
WORRY	91
THE SWARM	95
WINGS OF EAGLES	105
TRAPS	107
KILLING	111
THEY'RE BA-ACK!	117
STINK BUGS	125

WORDS	129
HEART'S DESIRES	133
INTEGRITY	137
HELL	141
NAUGHTY LIST	145
TEMPTATION	151
THIRST	155
PARENTS	159
CHOOSE YOUR BATTLES	165
SNAKES	169
FRUIT OF THE SPIRIT	177
INVITATION	183
ABOUT THE AUTHOR	187
ENDNOTES	189

INTRODUCTION

Years of seeing nature's beauty moved me to write this book. I'm not sure I would have taken notice of that beauty if it had not been for my husband who was an avid hunter and outdoorsman when we met. The many deer, squirrel and turkey hunting and fishing trips that we embarked on gave me such an appreciation of nature. We can learn from its beauty and from all the animals that share this earth with us.

I realized our responsibility to take care of and be good stewards of what God created. I also realized the thankfulness that grew in my heart from each and every one of those hunting trips. Each time something would happen, whether it was on a hunting trip or in my own back yard, I would thank and praise God for what I just experienced.

When I read *Psalm 104,* poetry comes to mind as I read the account of God's created order that was written in *Genesis*. One of the themes of *Psalm 104* is appreciating and praising God thru His creation.

PSALM 104

Praise the Lord, O my soul.

O Lord my God, you are very great; you are clothed with splendor and majesty. He wraps himself in light as with a garment; he stretches out the heavens like a tent and lays the beams of his upper chamber on their waters.

He makes the clouds his chariot and rides on the wings of the wind.

He makes winds his messengers, flames of fire his servants.

He set the earth on its foundations; it can never be moved.

You covered it with the deep as with a garment; the waters stood above the mountains.

But at your rebuke the waters fled, at the sound of your thunder they took to flight; they flowed over the mountains, they went down into the valleys, to the place you assigned for them.

You set a boundary they cannot cross; never again will they cover the earth.

He makes springs pour water into the ravines; it flows between the mountains.

They give water to all the beasts of the field; the wild donkeys quench their thirst.

The birds of the air nest by the waters; they sing among the branches.

Introduction

He waters the mountains from his upper chambers; the earth is satisfied by the fruit of his work.

He makes grass grow for the cattle, and plants for man to cultivate— bringing forth food from the earth: wine that gladdens the heart of man, oil to make his face shine, and bread that sustains his heart.

The trees of the Lord are well watered,

the cedars of Lebanon that he planted.

There the birds make their nests; the stork has its home in the pine trees.

The high mountains belong to the wild goats; the crags are a refuge for the coneys.

The moon marks off the seasons, and the sun knows when to go down.

You bring darkness, it becomes night, and all the beasts of the forest prowl.

The lions roar for their prey and seek their food from God.

The sun rises, and they steal away; they return and lie down in their dens.

Then man goes out to his work, to his labor until evening.

How many are your works, O Lord! In wisdom you made them all; the earth is full of your creatures. There is the sea, vast and spacious, teeming with creatures beyond number living things both large and small.

There the ships go to and fro, and the leviathan, which you formed to frolic there.

These all look to you to give them their food at the proper time.

When you give it to them, they gather it up; when you open your hand, they are satisfied with good things.

When you hide your face, they are terrified; when you take away their breath, they die and return to the dust.

When you send your Spirit, they are created, and you renew the face of the earth.

May the glory of the Lord endure forever; may the Lord rejoice in his works— he who looks at the earth, and it trembles, who touches the mountains, and they smoke.

I will sing to the Lord all my life;

I will sing praise to my God as long as I live.

May my dedication be pleasing to Him, as I rejoice in the Lord.

But may sinners vanish from the earth and the wicked be no more.

Praise the Lord, 0 my soul. Praise the Lord.

Introduction

Isn't that beautiful! As you have just finished reading *Psalm 104*, my prayer for you is that you take more time to appreciate God's creation and what he gave us, not only to be good stewards of but to enjoy. I believe that in appreciating what God created, we in turn can appreciate the One who created it. We thank you God for your creation and all of its beauty!

God's Magnificent Creatures

THE BAT HOUSE

When my husband and I purchased an old brick farm house in the country we knew that we would have some mice. Although I was not worried because we had an indoor cat and figured she would take care of any that came in the house. As far as other critters, nothing ever crossed my mind except for the occasional raccoon, skunk, or possum outside. One mid-summer early morning, around 3 am, I awoke and started petting my cat.

Abby always slept right next to my pillow at night. Many a night when I could not sleep, she would always be there and usually I would whisper to her and ask her if she was awake. She would always make this little squeaking sound back for a response. Now I have been told on numerous occasions that our pets have no idea what we are saying. Will you ever convince me of that, not sure. I stopped petting her and all of a sudden, she got up very quickly, sat next to me, raised up on her hind feet like a prairie dog and looked toward the door. She immediately went under the bed. I am very in tune with my pets and knew something was not right. I lay there with my heart starting to beat just a little quicker and did not hear anything. I could not figure out what it might have been that scared her, wishing at that time she could talk.

    I did not get out of bed to investigate but turned on my back and lay there, listening. After a few minutes I heard a sound of what I thought was a big moth flying over my head. Thinking it was a moth, I even swatted in the air as the sound went by. I said out loud even though my husband was in snore land, "I think there is a big moth in this room." I turned over and switched the light on and sat up in bed and looked toward the door. By now Mark was awake and I could not believe what I saw. I looked at my husband and said, as if I had seen a ghost, "Did you see that, I think that was a bat." At that time, I knew why Abby displayed the unusual behavior.

    Within seconds the bat was back in the bedroom and as soon as it flew back out, Mark flew out of bed and shut the bedroom door. He had planned on going back to sleep and I of course could not believe his lack of concern for not only the both of us but for our bird dog who was in the living room in his kennel. I looked at Mark and said, "Oh no, you are not going back to sleep. We have to get this bat out of the house before you go to work and besides, we don't know where it will go and hide for the day."

Mark grudgingly put on his jeans and I stayed in the bedroom, occasionally peeking out of the covers. Mark headed to the living room to let Morgan out of his kennel and being a bird dog, Morgan thought this was the perfect opportunity to try and catch what he thought was a bird. The chase was on! I could hear Morgan running on our wood floors and since I did not have the courage to come out of the bedroom, I missed the opportunity to watch Morgan's response to the bat. However, I knew from the sound of Morgan running and the sound of him sliding into the walls, our wood floors had a few more scratches on them. Mark told me, Morgan jumped up on the couch as if to get closer to the bat and as the bat flew over Morgan, he jumped up and realized it was not a bird and then he wanted nothing to do with whatever was flying around.

Mark had opened both front doors from our living room to our enclosed front porch and he yelled to me that the bat had gone out on the porch, which we were able to shut off to the house. Mark had also opened the two doors to the outside from the porch hoping the bat would get the hint and vanish outside. I came in the living room with my heart still beating at a more rapid pace and we both stood at the front door looking on the porch as if we were at the zoo watching an animal display! I could not believe the speed and the gracefulness of this flying mammal as it flew back and forth and up and down like a pilot in an air show. Precision and speed are so vital to the performance and is what keeps the audience in awe. My husband and I were in awe and shock!

Before heading back to bed my husband looked at me and in an I told you so manner said, "You did not believe me, did you?" "What do you mean," I said. "Remember when I told you how bats can get in people's homes and you did not believe me, now do you believe me?" Part of me was speechless because I hate those, I told you so moments, even though he was right. Mark also had to add, "Wait until we get our first snake in the house." Of all times to bring a snake into the conversation, what was he thinking? This was enough to deal with!

We just had a new roof put on and one of the chimneys torn down, so we figured that is where the bat entered our living quarters. We were pretty sure the bat eventually went outside. Mark thought it might be a good idea to bring one of our fishing nets down stairs in case this happened again. The small net was put in our utility room, not even thinking it might be a good idea to bring the big net down stairs and keep it in our bedroom. About a month later we both were getting ready for bed. My husband was sitting on the side of the bed and as I walked in the bedroom, I noticed a big bug on the window. For a split second I thought it was outside because of the glare the outside spotlight shines on our bedroom windows. But when it started spreading its wings and walking backwards down the window, I knew immediately it was not a bug. I turned to Mark and said in an excited voice, "There is a bat on the window!" I quickly turned and ran out of the bedroom and told Mark I was going to get the small fishing net.

I came back in the bedroom with net in hand and quickly put it in Mark's hand. He looked at me and rolled his eyes and proceeded to go up to the window, where the bat walked right down into the net. After disposing of the bat, Mark told me he heard something earlier in the bedroom, but thought it was the cat. As many wives do, they like to tell their husband what they should do in certain situations and in this situation, I felt he needed to know for the next time. "If you hear anything in the bedroom or for that matter anything in any other room, PLEASE investigate," I told him.

My thoughts started to get the best of me. Oh my gosh when did that bat come down into our living quarters, was it the night before and we never heard it and it hid for the day and it came out when it got dark or did it just come down from the attic somewhere. What is happening? Mark also mentioned that we needed to bring the large fishing net down from upstairs, which we did right away and put both nets against the wall on Mark's side of the bed. I always thought that big fishing net was a waste of money, just to have for fishing in Florida. For some reason I was grateful we had the big net along with the small net.

Several months after that episode we took down the sagging dropped ceilings in the living room and dining room to see what was underneath and realized they were put up to cover up the original plaster ceilings that had cracked and deteriorated. It took several months to install new ceilings which gave open access to the attic areas. We both knew the chances of more bats were pretty high now that they had easier access into the living quarters.

Several nights we all slept in the bedroom with the door closed, not realizing until several months later that we had a hole in our closet ceiling that more than likely was an access hole for the bats to come down. When I say all of us, I mean my husband, the cat and our dog. That did not work out too well because every time Morgan would move in his kennel, his dog tags would jingle and wake us, or should

I say wake me up. We discussed not allowing the dog to sleep with us anymore and besides if he should get bit, he should be ok along with the cat who both had had rabies shots.

We knew the percentage was very small of a bat having rabies, but the thought of having one of the few animals who can carry rabies, flying around your living quarters in the middle of the night, gave me an uneasy feeling. I woke up in the middle of the night and had to use the bathroom. I flipped on as many lights on my way to the bathroom as possible, thinking if there was a bat or bats flying around, they would get scared and go back up into the attic where they came from. After finishing in the bathroom, I peeked into the living room and swore I saw a bat fly back up into the attic area. Immediately, I screamed for my husband and he came out of the bedroom to investigate and upon turning more lights on we saw and heard nothing. To this day, I'm not sure I saw what I thought I saw. The rest of that night was sleepless.

Bats have a way of creating unwanted stress in one's life. I was standing in the kitchen after the second episode and a fly flew by my head and I thought I was going to flip out. My heart started racing and my hands flew up in the air swatting at it to get away. I realized than I had post-traumatic stress bat disorder. We finally got the new ceilings back up and that brought with it some relief.

A year later and here we go again. I awoke to what I thought was a bird having a hard time flying over our bed and realized within a split second it was not a dream and I knew immediately what it was. I told Mark in a loud voice, "There is another bat in our room." I went under the covers and Mark got up, turned the light on and the bat flew out the door. Mark shut the door and told me it was outside the bedroom. Mark put his jeans on and grabbed the fishing net. Both nets were in their proper places now.

As he was doing that I came out from under the covers and saw that my cat Abby was still lying next to my pillow. I thought that was odd but figured she was getting used to these flying mammals. The minute I thought that, I heard the flapping of wings underneath our bed and Mark and I looked at each other at the same time with eyes wide open. Mark's eyes immediately went to the floor on his side of the bed and I leaned over to watch my side of the bed. Within seconds the bat walked out from under the bed on Mark's side and he was able to put the net right over it. I knew why Abby was still on the bed and not under the bed.

As my husband was disposing of that bat it let out a small screech and the only thing I could think of was that the other bat was going to hear it and want back into the bedroom. As Mark opened the bedroom door, he raised the fishing net just in time and the other bat flew right into it and at the same time I went back under the covers. Mark disposed of that one and put them both in the trash can. After all of the excitement was over, we both went back to bed with a little apprehension. As I laid in bed trying to fall asleep, but at the same time listening for odd noises, all of these thoughts went through my mind again.

Of course, I had to share them with my husband who was trying to get back to sleep, so he could get up and go to work. "Do you suppose those bats hit the ceiling fan and that is why one was under the bed and the other one was having a hard time flying?" "Do you suppose they landed on our bed at some point in time?" "Did they have rabies and that is what made the one sound like it could not fly well?" I knew I could not dwell on what might have happened and was just grateful that I woke up and heard the one.

Morning came not soon enough and with little sleep, Mark and I discussed the subject of rabies and maybe we should get these two bats tested, just to be safe. Since we put them in the trash can and it was summer, the chances of their brains being tested were not good because of quicker deterioration. I removed the bats from the trash the next morning and put them in a bag and in a container and put them in the refrigerator at the request of the health department, but it was too late. They could not be tested. I was hesitant about putting them in the refrigerator but they were dead and in a container with a tight lid. This was not the first time we had had critters in the refrigerator. When you are married to an outdoorsman, you will have the occasional Styrofoam cup full of worms for fishing bait and the occasional Styrofoam food container filled with crawdads for bait. On occasion you will open the refrigerator door and low and behold a lively crawdad or two will have escaped the container and is crawling around inside the refrigerator.

The health department recommended we both get rabies shots, because of having several in the house. My first thought went back to my childhood when my younger sister was bitten by a squirrel and had to endure a series of rabies shots. The family physician at that time decided it was not necessary for her to get them in the stomach, so they rotated and placed them in her arms and legs. No way was I going thru that! The man from the health department said the rabies shots now are much better than years ago and you don't have to endure that many. That still did not put my mind at ease and Mark and I both decided after much discussion it was not necessary. If one of us started foaming at the mouth, we would deal with it at that point in time! Humor makes things a little lighter and easier to deal with for me.

After having four bats within a two-year period and doing some research on the Internet about bats, it confirmed my suspicions of the probability of having a colony in our attic. I decided to call an exterminator and ask some questions about what they would do to rid our house of the rest of the bats. I have to admit the discussing of bats can stir up some not so pleasant emotions within me. As I explained our situation, the very patient and informative woman on the phone told me she thought we had a colony in our attic. No kidding, I thought, it does not take a rocket scientist to figure that one out. After hearing the no guarantee and several thousand dollar price, I thanked her and did not want to take any more of her time. I knew my husband would not want to spend that amount of money and I knew in my heart that it was too much also for something that was not guaranteed.

As I reflected on the past bat episodes, I could feel my anxiety level going up, so I decided to call my husband and discuss what the woman told me. Hoping that maybe he would think it was a good idea and having less bats in the attic would cut down on the numbers that came into our living quarters. It is amazing what anxiety will create in us, focusing on the need to get something fixed yesterday. After hanging up from my husband and him telling me the thousands of dollars for this was not worth it and although he was right, the rest of the day was consumed by bat thoughts.

For almost two years we had no bats, or at least we never woke up to any. As with the anticipation of an upcoming bat anniversary, I began to dread the months of June, July and August which were the months the bats would come into our living quarters and what I called bat season. For me this season brought sleepless nights, anxiety, uneasiness, fear, worry, and an abundance of stress. I kept telling myself if we haven't had any for almost two years then we probably won't have anymore. I was trying to think positive, but boy, was I wrong. Again, we were sleeping and I awoke to something hitting the screen, as you can tell by now, I am a very light sleeper.

My side of the bed is about two feet from our windows and having no air conditioning we always slept with the windows open during the summer. The bats thought that was a way out and could sense they were close to the outside. They always seemed to congregate in our bedroom, which would have been the only windows open at night. I just happened to be lying on my side facing the windows and upon opening my eyes I saw something fall off of the screen. I thought it was outside and then my post-traumatic stress bat disorder kicked in. I positioned my body to almost lying on my back to be able to see something flying. With covers pulled clear up to my neck on a hot summer night, it did not take long at all for me to start sweating.

Within a couple of minutes there it was, oh my gosh, another bat. I hollered at my husband, "Mark, we have a bat." He lays there and said, "Why do I always have to get them." and I responded in a harsh manner, "Because you are the man of the house." I went under the covers and could hear Mark getting up and gathering the bat gear. I started becoming very claustrophobic and sweaty under the covers and wanted to yell out what is taking you so long, but knew it was my unwanted anxiety that would be talking. He captured the bat and hollered there is another one flying around the living room. I could hear Mark opening the enclosed front porch doors and the bat flew out on the porch and then could hear Mark running to both doors slamming them before the bat came back in the house.

My anxiety took over and I am telling him, "I can't believe you did that." He is looking at me with these sad puppy dog eyes and I continued with, "You know that bat is going to go back up in the attic from the porch and it will eventually come back down." By then, with more construction, the bats now had access from the front porch back up to the attic. I could have screamed and the minute I looked on the porch to see if it was still out there, my heart sunk because it had disappeared, probably back up to the attic. I kept on like a broken record, "You know we are going to have to shut the porch doors as soon as it gets dark and what if I open the porch doors during the day and it comes out?" Mark turns to me in a sharp tone and says, "Then you will have to deal with it." Then he very nonchalantly says, "Wait till we get our first snake in the house."

Of course, I had heard that one before after the first bat episode and felt it was very inappropriate to bring the snake up again. I could not believe what I thought was the insensitivity to not be concerned that he would allow this to happen. As the days went by, I had a difficult time sleeping and every time I opened the porch doors for some fresh air, I wondered if there was a bat waiting to get out. About a week and a half went by and so far, no bats. But then one morning as I got up, as the sun was rising, I felt it was safe to open the porch doors.

Why not? It was day light out. Did I watch too many movies back in the day? I made my coffee, started my day, and Mark got up and started his day. He was on a different shift and did not have to go in until mid-morning. I was in the bathroom primping and he was sitting in his chair in the living room reading the paper, drinking coffee, and watching the morning news. When all of a sudden, I hear stomping on the floor and groaning. I run out of the bathroom and Mark met me in the hallway all stooped over.

In a concerned voice I asked if he was getting sick and he yelled at me, "No, there is a bat." I ran to the back door to open it and our dog is chasing the bat. By now my husband was standing at the door to the front porch as I was entering the dining room. I could not believe the flight pattern of this bat. All of the others had flown up high, but not this one. This one flew very low, so low it flew under the dining room table that has two large pedestals underneath to support the table top. You know, those Amish made tables? Then it would fly close to the ceiling and with no warning back down close to the floor.

My husband just stood there and watched it and the expression on his face said it all. I knew what he was thinking because I was thinking the same thing. How are we going to catch this one? Or should I say, how is Mark going to catch this one? Everything happened so quickly, I don't remember who grabbed the net. It felt like it took forever to capture that one and as soon as it was in the net, I could not help myself and asked my husband, if he saw where it came from. He said, "No," in an abrupt voice. I will have to say I was impressed with that bat and his ability to fly with such speed, grace, and agility, especially going under the dining room table several times.

Just a couple of days after that I noticed what I thought was mice poop on our front porch on the concrete floor. Upon looking at it closer, I realized it was bat poop. When does this stop! I knew our bats in the barn left piles of poop wherever they roost. Mark was at work and I took a ladder and climbed it so I could see between the rafters and plywood and sure enough there is a bat. When Mark arrived home, his Sheridan pellet gun came out and he was able to get this bat. As of writing this we had 9 bats come down into our living quarters within a five-year period. We finally got smart and plugged the hole in our closet and since doing that have had no more flying mammals in our living quarters for over seven years. We have looked up in the attic on numerous occasions and have never seen a bat hanging or hiding and have only found three dead bats in the attic. As the years have gone by, I have become a little calmer during June, July and August. Just a little!

Throughout all of our bat episodes Mark always made me feel, with words, tone of voice and rolling of eyes, like he could not believe I was responding in such a way and how could I be afraid of such a small mammal. Have you ever looked at a bat up close? Yikes! I with my post-traumatic stress bat disorder also did not respond with patience and never thought before I spoke most of the time. However, after some squabbling back and forth, I found out he was not at all fond of these flying mammals, especially since he was the one capturing and disposing of them. It was just as upsetting to him as it was me. You would have never known it because of his responses to me.

Sometimes people's responses are not always appropriate and can be very hurtful. Things aren't always what they seem and many times people are hurting, afraid, or are just as broken as we are. We need to use our words with restraint and think before we speak. We need to be patient with one another and when someone offends us, we need to forgive them. We need to love them, not judge them.

"A man of knowledge uses words with restraint, and a man of understanding is even tempered. Even a fool is thought wise if he keeps silent, and discerning if he holds his tongue."
Proverbs 17:27-28

"The tongue has the power of life and death, and those who love it will eat its fruit."
Proverbs 18:21

"Forgive, and you will be forgiven."
Luke 6:37

EXPECTATIONS

We are awakened by the sound of our alarm at 4:00 am on the morning of November 27, 1995. This is not just any morning; it is the first day of whitetail deer season and my first-time deer hunting. As the alarm sounds, Mark, my husband of ten years, barrels out of bed, with the excitement of a child on Christmas morning. I slowly rise out of bed, anxious to get to our hunting area, but dreading the elements that we might have to conquer. The hour and a half drive to our hunting ground is filled with silence. The both of us are planning our own special strategy in our minds for the day's events, not letting the other opponent know what that might be, like General Patton in World War II.

As we arrive at our hunting spot, I anxiously, but quietly ask Mark, "What time is it?" He responds in a whisper as he is getting out of the truck, "It's about six o'clock and we have fifty-seven minutes before legal shooting time, let's go, Mary!" We quickly put on the remainder of our hunting gear that is piled up in the enclosed bed of our pickup truck. The camouflage coveralls, orange hunting vest, and orange knit cap that I wear, add an extra layer of warmth on such a frigid fall morning. Mark is dressed in a fluorescent orange hunting coat, pants to match that are held up by orange suspenders, and an orange ball cap. He has the look of Elmer Fudd, but the strength and skill of a sharp shooter.

We each load our own shot guns with deer slugs, flip on our small Maglite flashlights and start our trek into the woods. The leaves underneath our feet are like walking on open bags of stale potato chips. There is a light misty fog in the woods, which gives a certain eerie feeling. Mark is our guide and I follow several feet behind him. When the sounds of the woods start coming alive, I pick up my step and practically walk on his heels. Mark picks the spot where he thinks our trophy buck will appear.

We get settled in our positions, like soldiers getting ready for battle. I am sitting beside a large oak tree on the side of a steep hill and Mark is sitting behind and to the side of me, about ten feet away. As the first light of morning appears, I stand and scan the ravine at the bottom of the hill with my eyes only, careful not to move any parts of my body. There is a small creek bed in the ravine and hopefully this portion of the creek will quench several deer's thirst today.

Expectations

I start to scan back and Mark says in a whisper, "Mary." I notice the tone and quickness of the whisper and I quickly turn, knowing that he sees something. Eagle eyed Mark points toward the ravine and I slowly turn my head toward the direction of his finger. About seventy-five yards away from me through the thick brush, I get a glimpse of a buck walking by. He is oblivious to what's going on around him.

The anticipation and excitement of the morning finally hit me. My adrenaline started to pump more than I wanted it to. As I raised the shot gun, I could feel my heart pounding in my head, as if a time bomb was about ready to explode. I started getting a case of the dreaded buck fever, which every hunter experiences at least once and others get it every hunting trip. Buck fever is when you start excitedly shaking. I took a deep breath hoping to calm my shakes, aimed and pulled the trigger. The sound of the gun was like a loud boom that you hear on the fourth of July. I see a flash at the end of the gun and the next thing I know, I am sitting on my behind. My footing was off and the kick of the gun knocks me flat. I quickly get back up hoping for another shot, but know I haven't come close because of the fall and know the deer is long gone.

When I confirm that, I turn to Mark and his eyes are as big as saucers and his mouth is open wide, as if he has seen a ghost. In a jovial voice he says, "I have never seen anything like that before, are you ok, Mary?" I am speechless and can't believe what just happened to me. I burst out with laughter and Mark quickly joins in. After the both of us finish laughing at my antics, I quickly get myself back together and in position for another opportunity to try out my shotgun skills. Hoping that while getting ready, our laughter and excitement had not alerted the other deer's close by.

Within no time at all I hear the rustling of leaves behind me, up and over the hill. I move very slowly waiting to identify and see the source of the noise before raising the shot gun. All of a sudden, another smaller buck comes dashing over the hill right toward me. Because of the speed at which he is running, I know he is running from another hunter. He stops within fifteen yards of me, raises up, and looks into my eyes. I have never been that close and face to face with a deer before. He has big brown eyes and a look of doom on his face. All of a sudden, I feel sorry for the deer and cannot even raise my shot gun to try to shoot. As soon as his eyes met my eyes, he turns and takes off back up the hill. Within seconds he is gone and I miss another chance. Mark says with a stern voice, "Why didn't you shoot him, you had a perfect shot." I say in a monotone voice, "You should have seen the look in his eyes."

I say nothing else and position myself again, wondering if I have what it takes to be a hunter like my husband. I sit and lean against the oak tree, this time closing my eyes and thinking about what I might have done differently to have bagged one of the two deer. After several minutes, I open my eyes and twenty yards away from me stands at least an eight-point buck, grazing for food. I slowly stand, but try to make as little movement as possible. While I am raising the shot gun, buck fever hits me again. I aim and pull the trigger. Not knowing if I hit the buck for sure, I cock the gun and shoot a second time as he is running away.

Mark and I wait about twenty minutes before heading in the direction that I shot at the buck. When we reach the spot, we see no signs of blood or clues that the buck went down. I stand there in dismay, while Mark is more optimistic and searches a bigger area. Within ten minutes as we are still looking, Mark yells, "Mary look out!" Not knowing which direction to look, I stand still and within seconds a doe bolts by me, within five feet of where I am standing. I watch in shock as she frantically disappears into the brush, knowing how close I came to being trampled. The next thing I know Mark is standing beside me asking if I am ok.

It is almost late-morning and by now some deer start to bed down for the day, like a toddler who takes a rest period during the afternoon. The chances of us seeing another deer are very slim, the later it gets. We decide to call it quits. The drive home is full of conversation and a replay of the morning's events. Mark thinks the morning was fantastic, because we saw four deer within four hours. Even though I did not shoot one. I think the morning would have been fantastic, if one of those bucks could have accompanied us back home. I am going to shop around for a gun that does not shake for the next several seasons.

We all have expectations of how our lives and certain situations should end up. Have you heard of the expressions, It's not about the journey, it's about the finish line or It's not about the finish line, it's about the journey. In the Christian life I believe it's about both. During the journey we are to live life with a change of heart that comes with salvation. We are to have expectations in the promises that God has given us. We are to revere God in our daily lives and our goal should be to accomplish God's will for our lives and want to be more and more like Jesus everyday so at the finish line we can hear those words, *"Well done, good and faithful servant."*

Matthew 25:2

"Brothers, I do not consider myself yet to have taken hold of it. But one thing I do: Forgetting what is behind and straining toward what is ahead, I press on toward the goal to win the prize for which God has called me he heavenward in Christ Jesus."

Philippians 3:13-14

LITTLE CHURCH MOUSE

There are pros and cons to having cats and one of the pros are rodent control. All of our cats (5, not at once) with the exception of one have been indoor/outdoor cats. Living in an old farm house presents itself with the occasional indoor critter, bats, mice and snakes. Yes, I said indoor. Obadiah or Obie for short, (thought I might try a Biblical name on him), loves to hunt and has never found a mouse inside the house, even though we hear them in the attic at night. Never a dull moment at our house! I think the mice are smart enough to know what roams around on the main level and they stay upstairs.

However, Obie is constantly bringing his outdoor catch up to the back door for approval and praise. One afternoon I was not paying much attention and just happened to look down at him through the storm door window before opening the door. I noticed a tail hanging out of his mouth. I cracked the door and called out his name in a disappointed manner and told him "No" and closed the door. He dropped the mouse, looked up at me, picked up the mouse again, and flipped it high into the air. By the time he brought it back up to the house it was dead.

As a cat's instinct kicks in, they play with their prey until it is either time to eat it, discard it or leave it lay.

After this incident I told my husband, PLEASE be careful when letting Obie in and make sure he does not have something in his mouth. On numerous occasions Obie would come running with something in his mouth and always bring it to the back porch or up to me while working in the yard. Instead of complaining and yelling at him, I started praising him using a different tone of voice and telling him he was such a good boy for catching something, but only when we were in the yard and not at the back door. He would always drop it where I could see it and continue on with his prey. I wanted him to learn that he would get praise and petting when we were in the back yard, but a reprimand and a closed door when he was at the back door trying to come in the house with a mouth full. Not sure that psychology works with a cat.

One evening, late around 10:30 pm it was raining hard and I went to the back door to call Obie in for the night. I flipped on the back porch light and looked out the back door. He was standing with his head down, waiting to get in and I noticed he was quite wet. I quickly thought about a mouse, but with it raining and the rain blowing against the back door, I wanted to let him in quickly and get the back door shut. I thought there is no way he would have a mouse on a night like this. Obie came running in and as I shut the door, I turned my head and looked toward him as he was entering the kitchen from the laundry room. I saw nothing but a tail hanging out of his mouth. That call of disappointment came immediately out of my mouth and he dropped the mouse and that little mouse was alive and well.

    The mouse took off running to one of the corners underneath the kitchen cabinets and was sitting there looking at the both of us. I said out loud, "Oh, it is a church mouse, how cute!" The mouse was going back and forth looking at me and looking at Obie as if saying to the both of us, please let me go and especially don't let that black cat get me. That lasted for about 3 seconds and the reality that we had a rodent in the house brought on an urgency to capture and get it back outside. I stood at the kitchen/ living room door and hollered for my husband who was in bed. I was in a walking boot and on crutches, recovering from foot surgery. Getting around could be a challenge trying to catch a mouse, so I figured if I had help, we could catch this mouse and have a live release. My husband hollered back in a frantic voice, "Where are you?"

I knew he thought something had happened to me and I hollered back that I was ok and that Obie had brought a live mouse into the house. As my husband came down the hallway, I was standing in the kitchen/ dining room door making sure the mouse did not go out of the kitchen. My husband approached me, and I moved back into the kitchen, and the mouse was gone, Oh no! I told my husband it had to have gone in a hole underneath the cabinet front. Upon further searching from my husband with a flashlight and pole, it was a good assumption. My husband pulled everything out of the lower cabinet and Obie went right in and we then knew the mouse was somewhere in the cabinet. There was a crevasse between two cabinets and the mouse was hiding in that, but by the time my husband retrieved something else to get the mouse out, the mouse was gone.

My husband's suggestion was to leave the cat out in the house all night and maybe he would catch it again. My first thought was if Obie does catch it again, he will bring it into our bedroom and drop it on the bed for us to see, alive or dead. No way! I was not going to be awakened with something running across and or under the covers or waking up to a mouse who had lost its life and was starting to smell. Mark also suggested we put Obie in the cabinet and shut the door for the night. I didn't think that was a good idea either. We would have woken up to a scratched-up cabinet door and knowing Obie, he would have let us know during the night with his vocal meows that he was not happy being confined. Also, a mess in the cabinet from not being able to use a litter box, was possible.

After a few minutes my husband went back to bed and Obie lost interest in trying to catch this mouse. Obie went back outside and I found a trap to set in the cabinet overnight. I have always had good luck with peanut butter on a trap so that was my choice of bait. The trap was set, went to bed, and no mouse in the morning. I left the trap for a second night and still no mouse. On the third day, we took the trap out and Mark crawled back into this corner cabinet with a flash light and saw that the mouse had other areas to escape. We never found that little church mouse. When I say church mouse, that is what I call this variety of a house mouse. They seem to be shorter, have bigger ears, long whiskers and have the cutest face. That is the second time Obie had brought a mouse into the house. Thank goodness the first one was on my husband's watch and that one was caught quickly! This is why we don't have a cat door!

As parents you might not like certain behaviors that come from your children. Discipline is an important part of showing love to them and we can still love them unconditionally as God loves us while working on those certain behaviors.

"He who spares the rod hates his son, but he who loves him is careful to discipline him."
Proverbs 13:24

"Do not withhold discipline from a child; if you punish him with the rod, he will not die. Punish him with the rod and save his soul from death."
Proverbs 23:13-14

"Fathers, do not exasperate your children, instead, bring them up in the training and instruction of the Lord."
Ephesians 6:4

LIGHT VERSUS DARK

Before purchasing a story and a half brick farmhouse that was built in 1887, we were aware of some termite damage in the basement. It had been repaired, but we did not know the extent of damage in other parts of the house, including the very difficult to access crawl space. We had two different termite companies come out about six months after we moved in and they failed to see several areas that had quite extensive damage to several of the floor joists in the crawl space and both companies came to the conclusion, we had no termites. One floor joist was so badly damaged, my husband was surprised it had not failed. We did not have a home inspection and bought the house "as is." Will we ever do that again, probably. That's us!

The conditions had been and were perfect around the house for termite colonies to take up residence and for them to enjoy a feast of wood until their hearts content, with no one knowing they had moved in. Our 45' x 12' enclosed porch, which was across the front of the house, was finished on the inside and started getting this terrible odor. An odor so bad at times I would gag when entering the porch. Thank goodness we were able to close the porch off to the rest of the house so the odor would not permeate itself into our other living quarters. We could not figure out why it would smell that bad, so I decided to investigate further.

One corner of the porch on the drywall toward the floor was turning brown and I thought that would be a good place to start my investigative work. I have to say I kind of like demo work and with an eleven-inch drywall saw, I cut about a 6" x 6" hole in the drywall. Not only was the drywall easy to cut but on pulling it out it was soft, wet, and mold had started to appear on the backside. You could tell the porch had been leaking for who knows how long. I cut a much bigger hole and pulled some of the insulation out and it had been wet but it also had dead mice in it along with their droppings. The previous owner had put out mice poisoning on the porch and in the attic that we found. Decomposing mice smell is horrible, especially more than one. I also noticed something wrong with the 2' x 4's that I had exposed and as soon as my husband looked at the wood, he immediately told me I was looking at termite mud.

We decided to gut the whole porch to rid it of the mice infested insulation, which was probably most of the odor. However, we also knew that we would probably find more leaks and more termite damage. Upon further demolition, I could not believe the destruction that the termites caused. Upon completing the demo work it was clear and very disappointing that the termites had destroyed the whole porch, clear up to the edge of the front of the house. Leaving behind not just some, but a substantial loss of structural strength. Because of the rotted wood and termite damage, the front sill had shifted and was leaking. What a mess!

The porch, of course, smelled better but seeing all the termite mud and damage was shocking. Termite mud is tiny tunnels that the "worker" termites travel through from soil to wood. We have no idea how long the termites had been there and because they live in the dark you don't know they are there until the damage is done. The termite's purpose is to help the food chain by recycling wood for the soil. Amazing, isn't it? You want them to recycle the wood outside your house, not inside. After taking all the drywall off, trim, and insulation off, and pulling up the carpet we found evidence where they might have treated for termites at some point in time. We also found the design of the porch allowed water to gather on the outside front bottom sill and over time rotted the wood which made easy termite access from the ground to the wood. I felt like there was a neon sign out in front with the advertising slogan, "Eat for free here and stay as long as you like."

We can choose to be just like the termites and live in the dark which leads to a life of destruction or we can choose light and follow Jesus which leads to eternal life. When we reject or rebel against God, we choose to live in sin or darkness. When we accept Jesus as our savior, only through Him, can our sins be forgiven and our life be changed forever.

"I have come into the world as a light, so that no one who believes in me should stay in darkness."
John 12:46

"...I am the light of the world. Whoever follows me will never walk in darkness, but will have the light of life."
John 8:12

SONG IN OUR HEARTS

A couple of years after we purchased our house with 3.50 acres, I thought it might be nice to have a decorative but useful bird house in our back yard. I was somewhat hesitant because of our bird dog, Morgan. Even though we have three and a half acres and plenty of room for several nesting boxes of different shapes and sizes, I wanted one close so I could bird watch. I decided to visit our local bird shop which specializes in selling only wild bird items. After discussing my thoughts with this gentleman, he was pretty sure Morgan would not bother a nesting bird. Not sure now if that was just a sales technique or if he was truly being sincere. I like to think the latter. Or was I asleep at the wheel, knowing full well we had a bird dog.

The bird shop had a variety of bird houses and after much thought, I decided I would choose one that a wren would inhabit. I had my husband attach the bird house to an old sturdy fence post that was inside Morgan's fenced in area of the yard. I had no idea that a wren was such a beautiful song bird until one chose my newly purchased nesting box. I also found out quickly that Morgan liked to watch nesting birds, but his bird watching bordered on the definition of stalking and terrorizing. Wrens are 4" – 5" long, are brown in color, and are very energetic with such an effervescent song. These little wrens seemed to stay lower to the ground and hung out in low tree branches and bushes, but of course were never far from the nest.

As with many bird species the male and female wren take part in building and raising their brood. As soon as Morgan noticed them going in and out of the bird house, the pursuit began. Day after day he would chase the wrens and even started to jump on the old fence post. It got to the point where the jumping became so frequent and the post would shake so much that mama or papa wren would fly out and Morgan would begin the chase. Morgan would also stand next to the old fence post looking up at the bird house and bark and bark and bark, which would also create the same response of flight in the wrens. This continued until we put a four-foot-tall fence around and about two feet away from the old fence post and bird house. Morgan could no longer hit the fence post and although we tried to stop his unruly behavior, he continued to stalk the wren's, day after day after day.

No matter how much he terrorized them they continued to sing, day after day after day. The wrens come back every year and they have chosen several bushes in the yard to build their nests and seem to be determined not to let Morgan ruin their time here. That next year we decided to move the bird house outside our fenced in area to give the next nesting couple a break. The ones that nested in the bushes still continued to be stalked by Morgan and the wrens still continued to sing on a daily basis.

God does not promise us that life will be fair and that we will not go thru storms, persecution and the difficulties that life can bring in a fallen world. However, no matter what is going on in our daily lives we like the wrens can always have a song in our hearts, when we draw on the Holy Spirits power.

"Speak to one another with psalms, hymns and spiritual songs. Sing and make music in your heart to the Lord, always giving thanks to God the Father for everything, in the name of our Lord Jesus Christ."
Ephesians 5:19-20

"Let the word of Christ dwell in you richly as you teach and admonish one another with all wisdom, and as you sing psalms, hymns and spiritual songs with gratitude in your hearts to God.
Colossians 3:16

"O my Strength, I sing praise to you; you, O God, are my fortress, my loving God.
Psalm 59:17

FEAR

When Mark and I married, he was an avid hunter/ fisherman and I had never done either. Mark thought it would be nice for me to try squirrel hunting, so our first hunting trip was on public land. Wow, even though neither one of us shot a squirrel and my first attempt did not bag one, I could not believe how much I enjoyed this new sport. Walking up and down the hills and hollows was a challenge. I could tell pretty quickly how out of shape I was, but to be out in nature and the beauty of it all and the stillness at times was very peaceful to my soul.

After several years of squirrel hunting and deer hunting on public land, we decided to look for property that we could purchase that would allow us not only to squirrel and deer hunt but to hunt for turkey and grouse. We also hoped to use the land for camping. After a couple years of looking, we found the most beautiful 80 plus acres on a dead-end road in the hills and hollows of south east Ohio around the town of Glouster. Hunting seemed much more relaxed not having to worry about other hunters. Of course, we have had the occasional trespasser, who feels they are entitled to hunt anywhere, but having our own land has been a blessing.

After several hunting trips, following Mark into the woods before daylight, I thought it would be nice for me to go out on my own at some point in time. Gun season was in for deer and we were camping for several days hoping to bring home a trophy buck or two. It was during that hunting season that I decided to go out on my own. Mark decided to help me find a good spot to sit at toward the back corner of our property. Only after both of us had hunted for several hours with no luck.

We scoped it out and the place he thought I should sit was right by two holes in the side of a hill. I asked him if he thought something was still living in the holes and he said very confidently, "No." I was kind of uncomfortable about those holes and expressed my uneasiness, but also had confidence in my husband who had been hunting, trapping, and fishing since he was a boy. Plus, because of the view and what I might see coming from several different directions, I couldn't say no. It was decided that would be my exclusive hunting spot for the next day.

We got to bed early that evening in our 1970's, 28ft long, pull behind camper that we permanently put on blocks with a slanted roof addition over the whole camper. Getting to bed early was a rule of my husband the "drill sergeant." So we could get up and have time for coffee and breakfast, get our hunting gear on, and walk to our hunting spots before the sun started to rise. Sleep was scarce that night going over in my mind the path I would take the next morning. I knew I was going to be by myself in the woods in the dark with only a small Mag Lite flash light to light my path. It was also something I needed to prove to myself and to make my husband proud.

Morning came quickly and I was so nervous I could only drink coffee for breakfast. As we headed down the hollow, we barely said anything to each other. As we reached our early 1900's built barn, I knew it was time for me to head out on my own. We gave each other a kiss and we wished each other luck and off we went to our exclusive hunting spots. I crossed the creek in the lowest spot possible, walking on and over the creek bed stones. After reaching the other side I headed over to the logging road and up I went. Even though I had an old logging road to walk on part of the way, it was hard to distinguish the path at times with only a small flash light to illuminate my steps. I had about a

30-minute walk ahead of me and I had to call on Jesus numerous times.

It was a cold morning and with every breath, you could see the steam coming out of my mouth. I had several layers of clothing on, long underwear on top and bottom, then came a long underwear turtleneck and a wool sweater with a pair of jeans to almost finish my outfit. Had a very thin pair of socks on with wool socks on top of them and heavy boots for cold weather. To finish my attire, I put on camouflage coveralls with an orange hunting vest, orange winter hat and camouflage gloves. I also took with me a back pack with Kleenex in it for a cold runny nose, a thermos of coffee, and a knife. A camouflage color cushion with a strap, so I could hook it around my waist and upon sitting, it would be right underneath me to keep some of the cold damp ground from seeping into my body so quickly. Of course, I carried my 12-gauge camo color shot gun that my husband had bought me.

As I headed out on my own my nerves and thoughts started taking over to the point where I swore, I heard Big Foot or something that was watching and stalking me. I stopped and listened which only made things worse. Standing and praying but still listening, the unknown noises surrounded me and seemed to come closer at times, almost deafening. It is amazing what our imagination can conjure up. As I continued on the logging road, all of a sudden, I heard a branch snap as if someone or something had stepped on it. My thoughts again went to thinking the worst and was wondering if I would make it back to my exclusive hunting spot. Would something or someone get me and would my husband be able to find me if I did not come back. Would I fall into an old hidden well or could the ground just open up and I be gone.

It got to the point where I almost could not go any further but there was no way I was going to turn around and go back. I was not going to cry uncle. I stopped again and said another prayer and then started thanking God that I was able to make it this far. I continued on but with prayer and praise in my mind until I got to my spot. I felt calmer by the time I reached my spot and it seemed like it took no time at all to reach the area I was going to get my trophy. I saw the two holes in the side of the hill and decided to sit about five feet away from one of them, since my husband was pretty confident nothing would be coming in and out. I took my back pack off and sat it next to me and positioned my gun across my outstretched legs.

The sun was just beginning to peak it's head up and seemed like it took longer to appear when under the canopy of a forest. All of a sudden, I heard a noise and knew something was coming my way but knew it was too early to shoot a deer. As I adjusted my head somewhat in the direction of the noise, I realized it was coming across the ground.

I started getting a little nervous because I could not see with clarity what was coming but it was definitely headed my way. My thoughts went to the holes and as the critter got closer, I saw some white on it. I moved just a little and cleared my throat so the possum, no, SKUNK would know I was there and not surprise it. Wanted to scream out my husband's name but figured that might be a bad thing for me and I did not want a sample of the perfume that would be sprayed in my direction. Plus, I knew Mark would never hear me. I felt my heart pounding in my head as it got closer and prayed, "Lord, please do not let that skunk spray me." The skunk had other plans in mind and I do not think it saw me but was headed back to its home in the holes probably to sleep for the day. Thank goodness it decided to enter the hole farthest from me.

I sat frozen, holding my breath. After realizing what I was doing and since I knew it was in the hole, I would probably be ok. Just to make sure, I slowly picked up my back pack and shot gun and moved a little distance from the skunk's residence. I tried to get myself settled and back into the deer hunting mode but every so often I would look over to the two holes to make sure nothing was exiting them. No deer was heard or spotted that day but because I was so focused on what might happen if the skunk comes back out, I could have easily missed the opportunity to see a deer.

When our fears become so intense, to the point it affects our lives, we need to ask ourselves, where that fear is coming from. Fear can sure rule and ruin a life even if not only for a short period of time but for a life time. How many things do we miss out on because of fear?

"For God did not give us a spirit of timidity, but a spirit of power, of love, and of self-discipline."
>*2 Timothy 1:7*

"You will not fear the terror of night, nor the arrow that flies by day."
>*Psalm 91:5*

"God is our refuge and strength, an ever—present help in trouble."
>*Psalm 46:1*

THE COMFORTER

Cat lovers know that every cat has his or her own distinct personality. Never thought we would have a feline who would pester you until you picked him up, held him, and carried him around the house talking to him while he purred up a storm, kneading his paws. Many times, my husband or I would take him to the window and say, "Let's see what we can see out the window." My husband carries him around in a cradle position with Obie on his back looking up at Mark. I carry him in a burping position on my shoulder. One day I was carrying Obie around after his attempt to get my attention, came with biting at my ankles so that I could no longer ignore him. As we were looking out the window, I thought how nice it would be if I could be held, comforted, talked to and carried around and told that everything is going to be ok.

However, we are held, comforted and carried by our Heavenly Father and how much more wonderful that is. We do have a comforter who carries us when we become weary. We do have a comforter who is there to listen when we need to "bend an ear". We do have a comforter who has promised that *"he will never leave you nor forsake you" (Deuteronomy 31:8).* We do have a comforter who loves us unconditionally and gives us a peace *"that transcends all understanding" (Philippians 4:7)* in the midst of our trials. That comforter is called God, my heavenly father!

"But the Counselor, the Holy Spirit, whom the Father will send in my name, will teach you all things and will remind you of everything I have said to you. Peace I leave with you; my peace I give you. I do not give to you as the world gives. Do not let your hearts be troubled and do not be afraid."
John 14:26

"Praise be to the God and Father of our Lord Jesus Christ, the Father of compassion and the God of all comfort, who comforts us in all our troubles, so that we can comfort those in any trouble with the comfort we ourselves have received from God. For just as the sufferings of Christ flow over into our lives, so also through Christ our comfort overflows."
2 Corinthians 1:3-5

"Have I not commanded you? Be strong and courageous. Do not be terrified; do not be discouraged, for the Lord your God will be with you wherever you go."
Joshua 1:9-10

UNITY

Living in the country with farm fields surrounding us on all sides and fence rows thick with brush and trees, allows wild animals to roam freely without much urgency. We have seen coyotes, deer, foxes, raccoons, skunks, and opossums. I lost count of the foxes we have seen almost on a regular basis, especially during spring & summer. One humid summer day Morgan, our Brittany, was outside and barking like he had seen something close. I had all the windows open to the house so I heard him immediately and thought it was a red or fox squirrel that would jump from tree to tree in the back yard. Eventually getting to the tree that was their home within the fenced in back yard.

Did not think too much of the ruckus coming from Morgan because that tended to be the norm until the squirrel would disappear in the hole in a tree and Morgan would lose sight and calm down. After a few minutes I decided to take a look out the back door. Morgan's bark was a little deeper this time and not as high pitched. Scanned the fenced in yard starting to the left and looked over to the partially wooded fence line that definitely needed to be cleaned out on the far right. Morgan was running the fence line back and forth. The fence line was about 150ft long on the two sides of the yard. That was unusual and I thought there was a stray cat that I could not see that he was hoping he could get closer too, but it was not his stray cat bark.

    Stepped out on the back porch and took just a couple of steps out into the yard and by that time Morgan was up towards my direction turning and taking off back down the fence line at full speed. When he reached the end of the fence line, I saw a fox coming to the end on the other side of the fence. Could not believe what I saw and wanted to get a video or picture of what was happening. This had to be documented because no one will ever believe that I stood here and watched a fox run the fence line back and forth with our dog. Waited till Morgan came up close to my end so the fox would not see me and went back into the house to retrieve my camera and phone for a possible video and or picture.

    I went just a little further out into the yard and stood behind a tree hoping to conceal myself. I was hoping I was downwind from the fox and hoping I could get this on video or at least a picture of them. My hunting skills kicked in and I stood behind the tree thinking I needed camo clothes on and I needed to be closer to the brushy area on the fence line. I quickly snapped out of it and thought I had to do my best with what I had. I slowly peaked around the tree and they made one more run down the fence line, before stopping and looking at each other at the unwooded end of the fence. I still could not believe this fox and my dog were playing. Morgan's tongue was hanging out of his mouth and it was obvious he was getting tired, hot, and thirsty.

The fox did not seem to be bothered by their antics and seemed to enjoy having a somewhat different playmate. I went to raise my camera and the fox saw me. Morgan was oblivious to where I was and was not going to let the fox out of his sight. The fox, after seeing me, turned and ran up and over a pile of unsplit wood. I was disappointed that I had scared the fox away but knew this was not going to be easy. The pile was so high I could not see where the fox ran to and thought he had headed over to another wooded area behind the wood pile. I moved out from behind the tree and down the fence line and stood there out in the open watching. This little fox popped his head up and over the wood pile, like a Jack in the Box toy. The fox looked at Morgan and I and took off running.

I stood there and laughed at what I just witnessed and how much enjoyment that was for me to watch. Returning to the house, I brought Morgan out a bowl of water because he was determined to stay out by the fence in case that little fox came back. Morgan lay out by the fence for several hours just watching for his playmate to return.

Unity is such an important part of our lives, not only in relationships but church and community. It is so important to let go of the strife in our relationships and learn to get along with one another. As the phrase goes, "we can agree to disagree." People we think that we would never be close to because of first impressions, ignorance, differences, etc., can lead us to missing out on relationships that could have changed us for life.

"How good and pleasant it is when brothers live together in unity."
       Psalm 133:1

Unity

"Live in harmony with one another. Do not be proud, but be willing to associate with people of low position. Do not be conceited."

Romans 12:16

"I appeal to you, bothers, in the name of our Lord Jesus Christ, that all of you agree with one another so that there may be no divisions among you and that you may be perfectly united in mind and thought."

1 Corinthians 1:10

INSTINCT

As with all sporting dogs, if they are not exercised, a form of the terrible twos appears. So, being the proud parents of a field trial Brittany, my husband and I learned very early on how important exercise was to this wonderful creature. So, while my husband was at work, I was the one responsible for making sure a daily run was a part of our day. It was a walk for me, but a run at full speed ahead for Morgan. I am always amazed at what has been bred into dogs and how instinct kicks in. Brittany's are pointers who love to hunt birds, such as grouse, pheasant, and woodcock. Our fun-loving Brittany not only pointed birds, but rabbits, chipmunks, mice, and anything that was hidden in the brush. I had come to enjoy watching Morgan run with such excitement, knowing he was doing what he loved and was created to do.

One afternoon we headed out for his daily exercise on our 3.50-acre plot of land, with only about a half-acre fenced in. As soon as I opened the gate Morgan took off like a race horse. He headed toward our old and decaying 1900' s barn, which was an everyday event. He did not come out of the barn right away and he seemed to want to stay in the barn which was a little odd. We have chipmunks, stray cats, ground hogs, opossums, raccoons and other unseen animals that go in and out of the barn and I thought he was on a chipmunk or squirrel trail.

Morgan comes running out of the barn with his nose to the ground as if he is a blood hound. He runs around a small out building that sits about five feet away from the barn, stops at the side of it and points. He again takes off and does another circle around it at full speed. By then I headed back behind the barn around a grove of walnut trees. Morgan continued to keep his nose to the ground, running in and out of the barn and around the small outbuilding. The intensity of his hunt was apparent and I knew he was on the trail of something. He ran in the small outbuilding that housed a tractor and all of a sudden, I heard a lot of commotion. I thought for sure he was going to get a chipmunk.

I started heading to the small outbuilding and looked up and here Morgan comes out of the building caring an animal. I thought it was a cat and he shook it like there was no tomorrow. Because he had it in his mouth, I failed to see the white stripe running down its back. My first instinct was somewhat correct, but don't think pole cats (skunks) as us rural people call them, are in the same family as domesticated cats. Thank goodness I was not close because I did not want the pungent smell, to put it nicely, hanging over me like Charlie Browns friend Pig Pen. Morgan dropped the skunk then dropped to the ground next to the skunk, trying desperately to rub the smell off of his face. Can't imagine what that must feel like or should I say smell like up close.

I immediately called Mark and in an apprehensive yet frustrated voice I said, "You are not going to believe what just happened on our walk." Mark knowing the hunting skills of a Brittany, or let me put it this way, of our Brittany and the tone of voice of his wife, guessed it right away.

Mark suggested I get the dog back in the fence and grab the shotgun and get back to the skunk and kill it. Being somewhat of a hunter I knew I could do that. However, I did not know how close I could get without me having to bathe in tomato juice. I knew the skunk was not dead because it would raise its head and look as if to see how close we were.

However, I thought it might be injured badly with the shaking it had to endure. It took me a while to get Morgan back in the fence because he was still trying to rub the smell off of his face and was not paying attention to my commands. Did not know how much the excitement blocked out what Mark had told me on the phone. As soon as I got Morgan in the fence and myself in the house, I had to call him back. He explained to me what gun to grab, the 12-gauge shot gun and how far I could stand from the skunk, 30-40 feet, hopefully downwind.

I loaded the shot gun and as I walked behind the barn, you would have thought I was walking in a possible firing zone. Not knowing if the skunk was still there, I sure did not want to receive the same spray of unwanted ammunition that my dog received. As I walked slowly, almost on my tip toes and looked around, I realized the skunk had taken off. I was somewhat disappointed that it was gone, because Morgan had not learned to stay away from these fragrance carrying animals and this was the second skunk episode in about a year's time. I felt our chances of this happening again were very high if I could not end the unfortunate way an unsuspecting animal protects itself, especially this one.

I knew the excitement was not over and knew what to expect next, but did not have my husband here to take over and I just assist like the last time. I decided this time I was going to try tomato juice instead of our last concoction of peroxide, baking soda, and liquid soap. A trip to Walmart was necessary! As some humans do, we have this ability to hope that no one is able to identify what situation one has been in. Hoping I did not smell, I started smelling myself on the way to purchase the tomato juice. I had one small area of odor on the end of my jacket sleeve, but decided I was on a mission and this little odor was not going to stop me. At the cash register, my lack of self-esteem kicked in and I had to tell the cashier why I was buying several cans of tomato juice. Knowing that if I did smell, he would know what the odor was.

    I sure could have used Mark's help, because Morgan knew mom would tolerate more than dad. Trying to bath him outdoors proved to be too much for me and he had to be brought indoors in the bathtub to complete the task. I put on an old hunting sweater, held my breath, picked Morgan up, and carried him as quickly as I could into the bathroom, knowing full well how the house might smell after. One might ask, why did I not leave him outside for a couple of days. Even though he is a hunting dog, he is an indoor dog and a momma's boy. When I pulled up to the gate after my grocery trip, Morgan was sitting at the gate shaking with his ears back and his head down. This was about the middle of October and it was not real warm out. We accomplished the task and after I coached Morgan back outside just for a few minutes, I took my sweater off and threw it outside. I lit a couple of candles, one in the bathroom for sure, threw the bath towels in the washer and brought out the bottle of Febreze. What a day!

We learned that it took several months for the odor to go completely away on Morgan. When he got the least bit wet within those several months, it really brought out those memories. Morgan's nickname was Skunkinator and as much as I wanted that to be the last skunk episode. I knew it might not be.

An animal's instinct is to follow what it has been wired to do, regardless of the consequences. Our human instincts will drive us to do things. We have the choice to be obedient or disobedient. Diligently knowing God's Word can become our instinct/guide.

"But these men blaspheme in matters they do not understand. They are like brute beasts, creatures of instinct, born only be caught and destroyed, and like beasts they too will perish"
2 Peter 2:12

"Yet these men speak abusively against whatever they do not understand; and what things they do understand by instinct, like unreasoning animals- these are the very things that destroy them."
Jude 1:10

"For the word of God is living and active. Sharper than any double-edged sword, it penetrates even to dividing soul and spirit, joints and marrow; it judges the thoughts and attitudes of the heart. Nothing in all creation is hidden from God's sight. Everything is uncovered and laid bare before the eyes of him to whom we must give account."
Hebrews 4:12-13

OBADIAH

Living in a rural area brings with it the unwanted stray cats and the occasional stray dog. We have had a total of six cats so far that we have taken in and the last five were strays. I have been fortunate to find homes for several others. One hot summer night I started hearing an animal cry. Having no air conditioning, we always sleep with our bedroom windows open. Being a light sleeper, I would always wake up to the crying sound and on some nights almost a howling sound. It was a sound of despair and I knew that all was not right with whatever this was. The sound seemed to travel around our property at night and I have to admit I was hoping it would go away, but it didn't.

After lying in bed listening, I knew it was probably a cat. After about a week of hearing this every night, I finally decided it was time to look around our property. Having an old barn and a small old out building, stray cats seemed to gravitate to those two buildings. I started walking around the property and saw a black cat run out of the barn. Went into the barn and looked around and noticed that something had been sleeping on a very small pile of matted straw. Went out the back entrance to the barn but walked very slowly and as quietly as I could. The black cat was sitting behind the barn and as I called to it, "kitty, kitty, kitty," it just sat there.

I moved closer and it started walking away. I just stood there and talked to it as if I thought it knew what I was saying. I had a feeling this was our night visitor and either someone had dumped it or for whatever reason it came to our house and decided to stay. From a distance it looked like an adult cat but looked a little on the thin side. Night after night it would cry and day after day I would go out and talk to it. At one point in time this cat started responding back with meows in different tones. After about two weeks, I started feeding it a little at a time. I knew full well once I started this care taking that it was not going to leave. I would sit on the ground while it was eating and one day it finished and would still not come to me and I sat there and asked, "Did someone not want you?"

The sound that came out of this cat at that moment was the night cry I was hearing and it was as if it understood what I had asked. There was a sense that came from that cry alone that this cat did not know what to do, that he/she was in a strange place and was lost, lonely and hungry. It stayed in the barn and would be waiting for me in the morning, sitting in the warmth of the sunshine, out by my husband's pickup truck, looking up towards the house. I would feed it, spend some time with it, and go about my day. Our dog Morgan did not like the fact that we had a stray cat hanging around and I knew if I did not acclimate Morgan to the newcomer, we would have horrible issues to deal with in the very near future.

I started the acclimation process pretty quickly and it took a good month before I felt safe leaving the cat and Morgan alone together. The cat felt more at ease around Morgan and would come in the fenced in yard but only while I was in the yard. I knew the probability of finding a home for this cat was very small from previous strays and I knew that shelters would put you on a waiting list for who knows how long and never end up calling you. I sure did not want kittens to arrive so thought the best thing to do was take it to the vet and find out more information on it. Male, approximately 1 1/2 years old, not neutered, and full of worms. We took the appropriate measures to make sure he would not father any litters, dewormed, and shots.

Thought a Biblical name would be good and Obadiah seemed to fit him well. We call him Obie for short and Obadiah when he gets into trouble. Obie worked his way into the house and gets along for the most part with our other cat who was also a stray, Earl. Every once in a while, I have to break up a cat fight in the house. Males can be extremely territorial. Obadiah has been a character and has brought us a lot of laughs. We both think he is part dog because when you call him for the most part he comes running. When my husband and I are out working in the yard, Obie will start vocalizing short meows to let you know he is coming. How fitting the name, I chose for this cat and did not realize it until I wrote this story. Obadiah means, servant or worshiper of the Lord.

How many times in life do we reach out and help someone in need? Do we see a need and meet it or do we see a need and tell ourselves someone else will help, I don't have the time. Are our television shows, social media, relationships, family, shopping, etc. more important? When we meet people's needs unselfishly, we are showing God's love to the one you are helping. Yes, it takes time and effort, but the rewards are so great!

"Do nothing out of selfish ambition or vain conceit, but in humility consider others better than

yourselves. Each of you should look not only to your own interests, but also to the interests of others. Your attitude should be the same as that of Christ Jesus."

Philippians 2:3-5

"If anyone has material possessions and sees his brother in need but has no pity on him, how can the love of God be in Him? Dear children, let us not love with words or tongue but with actions and in truth."

1 John 3:17-18

In reply Jesus said. "A man was going down from Jerusalem to Jericho, when he fell into the hands of robbers. They stripped him of his clothes, beat him and went away, leaving him half dead. A priest happened to be going down the same road, and when he saw the man, he passed by on the other side. So too, a Levite, when he came to the place and saw him, passed by on the other side. But a Samaritan, as he traveled, came where the man was; and when he saw him, he took pity on him. He went to him and bandaged his wounds, pouring on oil and wine. Then he put the man on his own donkey, took him to an inn and took care of him. The next day he took out two silver coins and gave them to the innkeeper. 'Look after him,' he said, 'and when I return, I will reimburse you for any extra expense you may have. "Which of these three do you think was a neighbor to the man who fell into the hands of robbers?" The expert in the law replied, "The one who had mercy on him. " Jesus told him, "Go and do likewise."

Luke 10:30-37

In this last scripture, which one would you be?

PERSEVERANCE

Living in a house built in 1887, you learn very quickly that there are so many cracks, crevices, and holes that allow different mammals, reptiles, and birds to be curious enough to investigate the opening, no matter where it leads them. My ears have become very tuned in to my surroundings inside our house. Some might call it a sixth sense and some might call it chronic anxiety from having numerous critters showing up in our living quarters.

Passing through the living room one morning I heard the sound of scratching behind the wood burner where the pipe goes into the wall. As my heart started racing, my first thought was either a mouse or bat. I continued on with my daily routine, but the scratching noise would not stop. I sent my husband into the basement to look in the crawlspace where the wood burner pipe comes out of the wall and travels upstairs through the chimney. He saw nothing and found nothing and heard nothing and told me maybe something came down the chimney pipe from the roof outside. However, he did not think that was possible and expressed that I might be hearing things. How many of us have heard that before?

Mark left to run some errands and I ignored the possibility that I might be imagining the noise. At some point in time, I went back into the living room and heard tapping on the glass door of the wood burner. I stopped dead in my tracks not wanting to look toward the wood burner and let my imagination go wild for a few unbearable seconds. I was about 10 feet away and to the side of the wood burner, thinking I might need to grab my anointing oil. I slowly walked toward the wood burner and the closer I got I walked out by about one foot so I could see what was tapping on the glass and to my surprise a bird was in the wood burner. Oh my gosh, how did that bird do that? I could not believe our two cats had not heard the noise. It did not take long before both cats were sitting in front of the wood burner trying to figure out what the heck was going on and how they could assist the bird out.

With my husband gone I thought I could make an attempt to catch the bird if I slowly opened the door, positioned a large fishing net over it so the bird could fly in the net. My attempts led to the bird almost escaping into the house and of course the cats were on high alert, hoping mom messed up and they had a chance

Perseverance

to catch it themselves. I gave up after several frustrating attempts and thought it would be best to let my husband use his hunting skills to capture and free this bird. For the next couple of hours, the bird kept tapping on the glass and turning its head as if to say, is anybody out there?

The cats kept guard in front of the wood burner and every so often would take a paw and reach out to touch the glass. When my husband arrived home, I handed him the fishing net and told him, he was the man for the job. By then Earl had given up hope and was in his kitty cube asleep. Obadiah was not going to give up and started meowing at Mark when he went to open the wood burner door.

After positioning the net over the door, my husband opened the door and wouldn't you know it, the bird found the little opening that had no net across it and flew out into the living room with Obadiah behind it. The bird flew onto a small desk, about 20 ft from the wood burner as my husband was behind the cat with the fishing net. I yelled at Obadiah like he was going to understand what I was saying. Mark raised the fishing net and quickly put it over the bird. Yes, it was caught! After pictures were taken, of course we had to have proof. Mark gently took the bird to the back door along with Obadiah following right behind him, meowing the whole way. Mark released the bird and no animals were harmed in the capture.

After releasing the bird, Mark assumed the bird somehow got into the cap of the chimney pipe, came down the pipe and made its way into the wood burner. Wow, the determination of that bird and it was not a small bird, we think it was a starling.

How determined are we in our daily lives and our long-term goals? Do we give up easily? Do we allow those tapes to play in our heads? I'll never be able to accomplish this. I'll never make it. I don't have enough talent. I was told I would not amount to much. Do we allow our thoughts and circumstances to override what the Word of God tells us? What if that bird had given up?

"I can do all things through Christ who strengthens me."
>   *Philippians 4:13*

"For nothing is impossible with God."
>   *Luke 1:37*

"Consider it pure joy, my brothers, whenever you face trials of many kinds, because you know that the testing of your faith develops perseverance. Perseverance must finish its work so that you may be mature and complete, not lacking anything".
>   *James 1:2-4*

LET YOUR LIGHT SHINE

After the excitement of purchasing our 1887 brick farm house, we realized part of the purchase was an emotional one, but it doesn't sink in until months later. After having central air conditioning in our city dwelling, it hit my husband pretty hard the first summer that we either had to endure those hot summer nights or install window air conditioners. My husband does not do well with heat and I love the heat. We installed ceiling fans in four rooms within just a couple years of moving in and put an oscillating fan on top of our dresser, directed toward our bed. Our house is about 50ft from the busy road on a curve, so for safety reasons, the only windows that stay open at night are just our bedroom ones.

If you can get past the noise of the occasional diesel pickup truck coming around the curve and flooring it as they come to the straight runway looking part of the road, night time can be pretty peaceful in the country. With the help of my outdoorsman husband, I learned the sounds of the night. The mating sounds of spring peepers (frogs), the mating sounds of toads, the occasional cat fight, the barking of foxes, the howling of coyotes passing through, the loud screech of the screech owls, and the unmistakable hoot of a hoot owl. We also hear those sounds that remind us of the cruel aspects of nature in the food chain and we also hear sounds we have no idea what they are.

Our bedroom has three 72" double hung windows, so each window allows 36" of some air movement, when the wind is moving in our direction. They also allow a good portion of light to come in, especially on those full moon nights when critters seem to move more readily. I love the majority of the night noises and find it soothing to lay in bed and look outside until I fall asleep. The only night noise I have come to despise is the donkey sounding noise that comes from my husband as he slumbers off to sleep.

As I lay in bed one hot, summer evening, the lightening bugs were everywhere no matter where you looked. They were in our yard, they were across the road in the field, they were flying over the road, they were flying low to the ground, and they were flying high. No matter where I looked their light shone bright. It reminded me of my childhood when we would get our empty Miracle Whip jars, poke holes in the lid and catch lightening bugs. Of course, no matter how much grass and one or two small sticks you put in the jar, by morning the light of the bug had either gone out or was not as bright and iridescent as the night before. And usually by the end of the next day their light was completely gone. Oh, those childhood memories.

Like the lightening bug, do we shine our light no matter where we go and no matter who we are around? Even in the midst of trials does our light shine brightly or do we dim it until things get better? Do our emotions affect our light? Do people know you are different or do you blend in with the world?

"You are the light of the world. A city on a hill cannot be hidden. Neither do people light a lamp and put it under a bowl. Instead they put it on its stand, and it gives light to everyone in the house. In the same way, let your light shine before men, that they may see your good deeds and praise your Father in heaven."

Matthew 5:14-16

"When Jesus spoke again to the people, he said, "I am the light of the world. Whoever follows me will never walk in darkness, but will have the light of life."

John 8:12

"For you were once darkness, but now you are light in the Lord. Live as children of light (for the fruit of the light consists in all goodness, righteousness and truth) and find out what pleases the Lord."

Ephesians 5:8

FOUNDATION

As a repurposer and second-hand person, if we have it to reuse or repurpose that's my first choice. After looking through a magazine one afternoon I found the cutest do-it-yourself outdoor storage box that looked like a house. It sat on a 4'x4' post about 5ft above the ground and the post had a cross section to hold garden hoses. Wow, I could make that with a little bit of help from my handyman husband! I made a trip to the barn and retrieved some old wood. My husband cut the wood, I sanded and painted the wood and to give it a unique look, my husband cut 2" x 4" pieces of thin wood so the roof would look like a shingled roof. My husband put hinges and a handle on the door. I decorated the front, adding a wooden initial R for Rogers to the door with some wooden flowers bought at the local craft store.

We decided to put all the garden hose nozzles in it and on the back of the house we hung the dog's pooper scooper. After about four years the house paint on the outside walls started peeling and the initial R came off along with the flowers. The roof held up good but the four walls were looking a little shabby, especially the front door. When you repurpose things, sometimes old wood, especially wood that has been in a barn for who knows how long, doesn't last as long as new wood. During one winter I walked by the laundry room window and heard this rat a tat tat, rat a tat tat, rat a tat tat.

I looked out the window and a small wood pecker was pecking the heck out of the front door. A good size indentation had been made and it looked like in no time a hole would be opened up. By the end of the next day a 1" hole had been opened up. I opened the door to see if the wood pecker was in it or any other smaller bird that had found the hole and decided to make a home for themselves. It was empty except for the assortment of garden hose nozzles that lived there. Even though the house was starting to deteriorate and probably will quicker, now with a hole in the front door to let the weather in. The foundation is still standing and with a little yearly maintenance on the house including plugging the hole, it will continue to last through all four seasons of weather.

What do you build your spiritual foundation on? Is it money, material things, relationships, jobs, vacations, social media, video games, shopping, television, etc. When the storms of life come can we hold up to hurricane force winds, floods, earthquakes, etc. Or do we crack under pressure, leaving multiple crevices where our foundation eventually falls. Or, do we build it on the rock, Jesus Christ! When building on the rock, we will be able to stand firm no matter what comes our way.

"Therefore, everyone who hears these words of mine and puts them into practice is like a wise man who built his house on the rock. The rain came down, the streams rose, and the winds blew and beat against that house; yet it did not fall, because it had its foundation on the rock. But everyone who hears these words of mine and does not put them into practice is like a foolish man who built his house on sand. The rain came down, the streams rose, and the winds blew and beat against that house, and it fell with a great crash."

Matthew 7:24-27

"For no one can lay any foundation other than the one already laid, which is Jesus Christ. If any man builds on this foundation using gold, silver, costly stones, wood, hay or straw, his work will be shown for what it is, because the Day will bring it to light. It will be revealed with fire, and the fire will test the quality of each man's work. If what he has built survives, he will receive his reward. If it is burned up, he will suffer loss; he himself will be saved, but only as one escaping through the flames."

1 Corinthians 3:11-15

"Nevertheless, God's solid foundation stands firm, sealed with this inscription: "The Lord knows those who are his, and, "Everyone who confesses the name of the Lord must turn away from wickedness."

2 Timothy 2:19

PURPOSE

In our neck of the woods, we call these birds buzzards, others call them turkey vultures. Our first encounter was when we were looking at our current property before purchasing and upon approaching the barn, three white tufted baby buzzards went running out of the barn with mom or dad right behind them. Wow, even as babies they have an odd look to them, so ugly, they are cute. As the saying goes, that's only a face a mama could love. Our property in South East Ohio brings a mama buzzard every year to our barn in which she lays 1-2 eggs and not in a nest but on the dirt floor. Buzzards for about the last ten years have been a regular part of our lives. Upon returning home one day to a road kill in front of our house, eight buzzards were sitting in the trees along our driveway while Obie (cat) was sitting in the driveway looking up and around at the buzzards.

Buzzards have almost a science fiction look, something you might see that was created for a sci fi movie. Buzzards migrate south for the winter and return in our area around my birthday, March 16th. Buzzards are social and the large groups of them we see circling over something dead are called wakes. Buzzards mate for life and the male and female participate in the raising of their young. Buzzards have a purpose, they eat dead animals and have a keen sense of smell up to a mile away. Buzzards assist us in keeping dead animals off the road and cleaned up in nature.

It does not matter what we look like, where we come from, who our parents are, how many siblings we have or don't have, where we grew up, where we went to school, what degrees we have or don't have, where we work, how much money we have or don't have, where we live, and the list can go on and on. What matters is WE ALL have a God given purpose on this earth and some of our purposes might not be so appealing to others but it's our purpose. It's up to us to find that purpose and do it to the best of our ability!

"For we are God's workmanship, created in Christ Jesus to do good works, which God prepared in advance for us to do."
Ephesians 2:10

Purpose

"Many are the plans in a man's heart, but it is the Lord's purpose that prevails."
Proverbs 19:21

"And we know that in all things God works for the good of those who love him, who have been called according to his purpose."
Romans 8:28

WORRY

It was the middle of February and we had had our share of winter weather. We already had about seven inches of snow on the ground and we were expecting another eight plus. The eight plus inches had started and we had gotten around three inches of it. I decided to start shoveling some of our 150ft driveway and because we were getting an inch an hour for several hours, I knew I would have to go out several times, to keep up with the light and fluffy snow. This was our first year living in a rural area and we had not purchased equipment to be able to remove an abundance of snow, so shoveling it was.

My second shoveling was right at dusk and with two flood lights that shone on part of the driveway, I knew I could shovel in the dark with no problem. For me there is nothing more serene than to be out in a snow fall at dusk when you hear nothing but the snow gently hitting your surroundings. As the snow continued to fall my surroundings became so beautiful with the snow starting to cover everything. Even the tooth pick size branches had a light dusting on them. The snow started to glisten in some areas where the flood lights interacted with each distinct snow flake. Everything looked so pure, clean, and untouched. It was definitely a winter wonderland!

As I am shoveling, I hear this noise, I stopped but the noise stopped. I continued shoveling but with slower movements and making sure I didn't scrape the shovel on the gravel. So, if I hear the noise again, I might be able to tell what it is and where it is coming from. I hear the noise again and I knew right away it had to be some type of owl. I looked up and around and see nothing and all of a sudden here flies this little owl, landing in a Ginko tree about ten feet from where I am standing. I knew right away it was a screech owl. Within seconds here comes another one and lands right next to it.

My first thought was male and female. One made this cooing noise and one took off flying and landed in a tree about 50 ft from where I was standing. The other one flew to another tree about 10 feet from the Ginko tree and landed on a branch, made another cooing noise and then went in a hole in the tree and I knew then that must be their home. Several years before that on a camping trip we heard a screech owl at night. My husband told me how small they were which was hard to believe for such a loud screeching noise which they produce. I remember asking God to see a screech owl before I died and sure enough that snowy evening, my prayer was answered. After that camping trip and before my answered prayer, I looked up screech owls to see what they looked like.

I thanked God for my answered prayer and then started thinking about all of the snow on the ground and how difficult it must be for them to find food. My heart sunk and as silly as it might seem I stood there and said a little prayer for the owls. I never saw those screech owls again but because of what the Bible says, I knew they would be taken care of.

How many times do we worry about life? Will we have enough money for just the basic necessities in life, food, shelter, clothes? Do we worry about tomorrow? Do we worry about our future and what might or might not come? Are we chronic worriers? Or, do we follow what *Matthew 6:25-34* says about worrying. Do not worry!

"Therefore I tell you, do not worry about your life, what you will eat or drink; or about your body, what you will wear. Is not life more important than food,

and the body more important than clothes? Look at the birds of the air; they do not sow or reap or store away in barns, and yet your heavenly Father feeds them. Are you not much more valuable than they? Who of you by worrying can add a single hour to his life? And why do you worry about clothes? See how the lilies of the field grow. The do not labor or spin. Yet I tell you that not even Solomon in all his splendor was dressed like one of these. If that is how God clothes the grass of the field, which is here today and tomorrow is thrown into the fire, will he not much more clothe you, O you of little faith? So do not worry, saying, 'What shall we eat?' Or 'What shall we drink?' or 'What shall we wear?' For the pagans run after all these things, and your heavenly Father knows that you need them. But seek first his kingdom and his righteousness, and all these things will be given you as well. Therefore, do not worry about tomorrow, for tomorrow will worry about itself. Each day has enough trouble of its own."

Matthew 6:25-34

THE SWARM

About the third year of living in our house, one day during the spring, I heard bees buzzing while I was filling a sprinkling can at the east side of our house. I stood still and looked around and then looked up and saw bees flying around the corner of the house on the second story just below the wood trim that is underneath the roof edge. It looked like some were going into possibly a small hole in the corner. I showed my husband and mentioned that we might have a bee colony in the house and probably in the wall somewhere. My husband told me we did not have a colony in the walls and to stop worrying about it. I was not worrying about it, I was just pointing out what I saw and thought. I knew his response was one of denial and he wanted nothing to do with trying to find out if his wife was correct.

I put the bees out of my mind and did not think about them until the next spring when I heard them again and saw they were in the same area but the number of bees flying around had increased. I knew then we had bees somewhere upstairs in the wall. I went upstairs to see if I could hear anything or see anything but there was nothing. A couple weeks after that I had been outdoors gardening and when I came into the house there were around 20 bees flying around the kitchen window and the dining room windows. As I was going around with a fly swatter, I noticed a bee coming out of a recessed light just above the kitchen sink. I did not know why they were coming down into the first floor. Then I remembered the year before I killed a few bees that were also in the kitchen and dining room but at that time thought they had come in from our enclosed front porch.

After getting rid of all the bees in those two rooms, I went upstairs to see if I could hear anything if I put my ear up to different areas on the wall. As soon as I entered the kitchen area upstairs, I heard bees buzzing and the window had around 15 bees on it trying to get out. This was mentioned to my husband when he returned home from work about what the bees had done. Again, he did not want to deal with the bees which created some tension and I was made to feel like I was whining and complaining about some little honey bees.

Trying to put the bees out of my mind, I got on the internet to look up bee behavior. I was hoping to find information that would calm my thoughts. Instead, I found information that said depending on how long a colony has been in one spot we could have thousands of bees in our wall. I tried to think of the positive and the only positive I could come up with was that we had bees to pollinate our fruit trees, etc. As spring and summer went by, I would go out and look up to see if the bees were still there and at some point in time during late summer, the bees only came to my mind on occasion.

The following spring arrived and here we go again. I was out by the hose and sure enough I heard the bees, looked up and their number had increased from the last year. Just like the year before, several weeks after that we had more honey bees that came down into our kitchen and a few in our dining room, at least 50. After getting rid of the bees in the kitchen I went upstairs and there had to be over 50 bees climbing all over the window trying to get out. Left the bees upstairs alone thinking if my husband saw that many, he would want to do something about the bees. Wrong! By the time he got home and I took him upstairs, all the bees had died on their own. At least I tried!

The bees started to really bother me for some reason and I thought it best if we found where they were and got them out. I found a bee keeper after much internet searching that did live removals and was willing to come out to look if we paid for his gas. The other bee keepers I found wanted more than gas money to come out and found the expense to have the bees removed was a little more than I wanted to spend for bees. The bee keeper came out and could not find where they might be in the walls even upon using a stethoscope placed in several places.

He suggested we drill holes in different areas where he thought they might be, hoping to drill into the honey combs. He also suggested we have tape ready in case we drill into the honey comb and we could put tape over the hole to prevent bees from coming out. He also thought that if the bees had been there for several years, we could have a substantial colony of thousands. I left it with the bee keeper that when and if we found the comb or combs, I would call him and he could do a live removal. The following weekend I convinced my husband to remove some kitchen cabinets (the upstairs use to be a full apartment) and drill holes into several places where the bee keeper thought they might be. We ended up drilling around 10 holes and in only one we saw bees in it but no honey comb. We had to tape over that hole pretty quickly because bees were wanting out.

My husband was getting irritated and kept saying we should have never drilled holes or take the cabinets down. I on the other hand, thought very differently. These were the old metal cabinets and had been up for years and were looking pretty tattered. Trying to keep the peace I said, "Let's leave this alone and maybe next weekend we can drill a few more holes." It got to the point where I was waking up at night thinking about the bees and how I felt we needed to get them out. We had more bees coming into the kitchen off and on and I was the one dealing with them. It got to the point where the bees were consuming my thoughts. I had become obsessed with the bees!

    I finally decided to give the bees to God. When I say give the bees to God I mean letting go of the situation and let God work things out. As soon as I gave the bees to God, I felt a peace come over me and I knew that to take the bees back would be wrong and that I would be telling God I did not trust Him with this situation. I also thanked God for how He was going to handle the situation. Several weeks went by and on occasion when getting water from the hose, I would look up and see what they were doing. One day I looked up and there were many bees starting to cluster together just outside their entrance to the house and I wondered if something was going on in the colony.

    I continued to go on with my days not worrying about our bee situation. With all the articles I read on the internet about bees, I learned so much about honey bees and their habits. It was a Saturday afternoon, late that summer and I was headed to the barn to look for a crate. Was not going to go at first but something kept pushing me to go out and look and not put it off. As soon as I got to the gate, I looked as I always did at a new flowering quince bush, I had planted between two older flowering quince bushes. That summer brought a slight drought and newly planted bushes need extra care even in a normal season.

As I looked toward the new bush, I immediately saw a large swarm of bees, something I had only seen in pictures. I did not go close because I was unsure of what they might do, but stood there for a few seconds watching them. Went back into the house to get my camera and took several pictures. Headed out to the barn and got the crate and on my way back, when I was about 20 feet from the swarm, it took off. Oh my gosh, it looked like a tornado forming backwards and then all of a sudden, they took off toward the tops of the trees and disappeared. Was that God nudging me to get to the barn, so I would not miss seeing this spectacular sight. My gut told me those were our bees, so I quickly went into the house and started searching bee swarms so I could know why and what they were doing.

My husband had been running errands, arriving home while I was on the computer. I told him about the swarm and what the article said and how we had a small window of time before a new queen hatched, in what was left in the colony inside our house. My husband rolled his eyes like here we go again with the bees. I knew in my heart this was God at work and I was not going to let anyone stand in the way of what God was doing and what needed to be done. I convinced my husband to drill a few more holes about an inch from the other previous drilled holes and sure enough the drill went into the comb and came out with honey on it. Halleluiah! Thank you, Jesus! My husband cut a hole into the wall and sure enough to our amazement there were four combs hanging with only a few bees left behind to manage the combs until another queen and more bees hatched.

After removing the four combs we found three more that we could only get to when we cut a hole on the other side of the kitchen in the bathroom wall. We put the combs in a five-gallon bucket and took them outside and laid them on newspaper. It was amazing to see the intricate and delicate looking combs and in quite a few of the holes, bees were starting to hatch.

We went back upstairs and made sure we had gotten all of the honey combs. The next weekend my husband got up on a ladder and filled all the holes he could find around the whole house with caulking so the bees would not come back and build again.

Now, that was God at work in this situation. When we turn things over to God and wait for Him to work in our lives things just seem to work out. God's timing is always perfect, we just have to have the patience and faith to wait on Him. We did not have to spend the money to have a bee keeper remove them, which saved us money. Things worked out great!

"Do not be anxious about anything, but in everything, by prayer and petition, with thanksgiving, present your requests to God. And the peace of God, which transcends all understanding, will guard your hearts and your minds in Christ Jesus."

Philippians 4:6-7

"Cast all your anxiety on him because he cares for you."

1 Peter 5:7

"Cast your cares on the Lord and he will sustain you; he will never let the righteous fall."

Psalm 55:22

WINGS OF EAGLES

It was mid-winter and returning from the thrift store which I like to frequent often, I was on the outskirts of West Jefferson, Ohio. I saw something large in the field ahead. This is mostly farm country with houses scattered here and there. Some new builds, original farm houses from years back, and a mix of years in between. As I got closer, I thought the only thing it could be was a buzzard, however, buzzards had already migrated a little further south for the winter and wouldn't be back until March. The closer I got, I could not believe my eyes. Is that a bald eagle?

I slowed down to almost a stop and it was eating a carcass of some kind. As I passed by, the eagle looked over at me. It looked so strong, confident, powerful, and majestic. It was beautiful and I had only seen eagles in books or on television before, never up close. Where was its nest, was it male or female, how far did it travel? What was it eating? I do know that eagles soar very high and out of all birds they probably fly the closet to the heavens. What a treat that was for me on that gloomy winter day.

I had to ask myself on the drive home, how high do I fly on a daily basis? Do I soar like the eagle in everything I do? Do I stay on the ground and never get air borne? Do I take off and then land shortly after? Do I only fly to a certain height all the time, fearful of climbing higher? I want all that God has for me and to fly like an eagle I have to constantly renew my mind, which in turn renews my strength and outlook.

"But those who hope in the Lord will renew their strength. They will soar on wings like eagles, they will run and not grow weary, they will walk and not be faint."
Isaiah 40:31

"Therefore we do not lose heart. Though outwardly we are wasting away, yet inwardly we are being renewed day by day."
2 Corinthians 4:16

"Who satisfies your desires with good things so that your youth is renewed like the eagle's."
Psalm 103:5

TRAPS

My husband grew up around Indian Run Creek in Dublin, Ohio. Over 60 years ago it was all farm fields. It is now known as Muirfield with multiple upscale housing additions and the world class Memorial Tournament held at Murfield Village Golf Club. Mark's father and uncle were avid hunters and Mark grew up with black & tan coon dogs and they also had a menagerie of animals around the house. A goat named Twiggy, dogs, horses named-George, Nipper (yes, he did bite), April, Wanita, Mayburt, and Tippy, chickens, pheasants, a sheep and a raccoon named Dinky. Dinky was found as a baby, accidently by one of the coon dogs. Dinky became a part of the family and was allowed in the house. However, the older Dinky got, the more mischievous he became. A wild animal has a difficult time becoming a house pet and when instinct kicks in even at a young age, havoc became the norm from Dinky, even in the house. Dinky would come and go and one day he never came back.

Mark got his first gun at the age of 5, a Daisy BB gun. At 6 he received a 22-bolt action single shot and at 8 he was given a shot gun.

He was taught how to handle a gun and was told that guns can kill people and he needed to be able to handle them with care. With supervision, he proved to his dad, he had the maturity and proper handling to be unsupervised. Squirrels, rabbits, and raccoons were among the first animals that he bagged. At the age of six his dad also introduced him to trapping on Indian Run Creek and a move to Ostrander, Ohio on Mill Creek at the age of 12, meant the trapping could continue.

    Mark's dad set the traps until Mark was strong enough to do it on his own. Mark would get up early before he went to school and check his traps. Mark's first catch on Indian Run was a mink, and he also caught muskrats, raccoons, foxes and the occasional, Oops! Mark also sold the furs, $2 for a muskrat, $3 for a raccoon and $12 for a mink. My husband is retired now and has not trapped for 60 years, but with more time available, the urge to take it up again has hit. As of writing this he has applied for his trapping license.

    As for me I am not a trapper but have felt trapped before in life's situations. How many times in life have we been trapped and can't get out? Trapped in drug addiction, alcoholism, gambling, abusive relationships, miserable jobs, children that have become unruly and thoughts of why did I have children, depression, loneliness, etc. How about temptations that we know are wrong but become too enticing to turn and run? Have we gotten out of a trap and fall back into the same one or a different one? Sometimes we feel trapped just in the everyday doldrums of life. There can be all different traps that we might experience in life. However, God provides a way out of our temptations and traps if we only turn to Him in pray for wisdom, guidance, strength, endurance and the ability to listen when He responds.

"No temptation has seized you except what is common to man. And God is faithful; he will not let you be tempted beyond what you can bear. But when you are tempted, he will also provide a way out so that you can stand up under it."

Corinthians 10:13

"And lead us not into temptation, but deliver us from the evil one."
Matthew 6:13

"The Lord is near to all who call on him, to all who call on him in truth."
Psalm 145:18

KILLING

I hesitated to write this story, however in nature and with instinct, whether God given or man's innate ability to continue to perfect certain breeds of dogs, tragic things will happen. Not always do things turn out for the good, however, it's a part of nature. As much as I adore my pets, they all come with unwanted behaviors. Some Brittany's, not all, stalk and kill and ours was one of them. I have heard people say that dogs are not supposed to kill other animals and if they do, there is something wrong with them.

That is far from the truth and depends on the breed whether they kill small animals or not. Morgan went after anything that moved and was a much better mouser than Earl (our cat). The difference is that Morgan attacked quickly and the end of life for his prey was very short and quick. Where Earl strikes but drags the inevitable end of life for the prey on and on with the game of strike and play or you could call it strike and torment. I have seen them both kill and it was not pleasant to observe but I have to continue to tell myself that is nature. It's a part of life!

When we brought Morgan home as a puppy, Abby (our cat) had the run of the house and as soon as Morgan came into the house and saw Abby, he immediately chased her and she took off upstairs. That only had to happen a couple of times and she retreated to the upstairs and would not come down. I was naïve and did not know I could acclimate Morgan to Abby and he would not chase her. Our master bedroom was upstairs so I had to bring her litter box upstairs and make some changes for her to live upstairs. She was upstairs for two years and when we moved, I had planned in my head how to set her up in our new home. To my surprise she was not going to be contained anymore in one room and she took over our new home. By then Morgan was use to her smell and they both lived in harmony.

I am amazed at how Morgan, if acclimated, knew our household cats from a stray cat. He knew not to harm a household cat whether it stays inside or outside but with no hesitation will pursue one outdoors that is not part of the household. With patience, I was able to acclimate Morgan to four cats which took several weeks. It was early spring, the sun was out and the creeping phlox was in bloom along with tulips and daffodils. The first of the flowering trees were in bloom, red bud and crab apple and the weather called for just a light jacket. The air was filled with that spring aroma of fresh grass.

On a Saturday afternoon, I prepared Morgan for his daily run. Mark usually took him on the weekends which gave me a break and allowed the two boys of the house some time together. However, Mark was busy working on the house and I decided to go ahead and take Morgan for his exercise. I regretted that run for weeks! Even though I always loved Morgan, certain behaviors were hard to swallow. After sitting at the gate and waiting for me to release him, I opened the gate and said, "Ok." I shut the gate and latched it. Morgan always headed to the barn first and in no time he had disappeared. I took just a few steps and heard this horrible cry and knew he had a cat.

I ran back in the house and as soon as I stepped in the door I screamed for Mark and told him Morgan had a cat in the barn. Mark did not believe me at first and said it is probably a skunk or ground hog. The look I gave Mark and the response after, told him not to disregard my call for help and that we both needed to get to the barn. Just a couple of minutes after hearing the first cry Mark was headed to the barn and I right behind him. When we stepped in the barn, I could not believe my eyes. Morgan had a very large male cat in his jaws shaking it and the smell of cat urine was overwhelming. We both stood there in shock and Mark was able to get Morgan to drop the cat which was by now probably dead.

Mark took a hold of Morgan's collar and escorted him up to the gate and led him in to the back yard. Of course, Morgan was wound up and ran the fence line back and forth looking toward the barn. I could not go back in the barn and Mark had the difficult task of making sure the cat was dead so it would not suffer anymore. It was too late to do anything for the cat, Morgan had killed it. When my husband came out of the barn, he said another cat was hiding in the barn underneath some wood. We kind of knew the reason for them to be in the barn and that they were probably loving on each other. The rest of the day I kept thinking about Morgan's behavior and how unpleasant the other cat's death was.

I struggled on how to end this story because we have so much killing in our society. The killing of people, unborn babies, more and more children are being killed by a relative or being taken by a stranger and killed, families are killing family members, etc. It does not stop!

Also thought about the behavior of us humans and how we have created such an unwanted, unnecessary surplus of stray and feral cats and what those consequences of those actions bring. In Genesis 1, God gives man dominion over all animals. That means we are to be good stewards and not abuse them or dump them because we don't want them. We have many behaviors that do not please God, but He still loves us unconditionally.

By killing/crucifying our flesh, that will change a lot of behaviors that we as humans have. When we follow Jesus, we can repent and ask for forgiveness for our behaviors and move forward with the hope and faith of not repeating those actions and become more like Him. When we renew our minds with His word, we allow it to penetrate into our hearts.

What is the condition of your heart? Have you thought about the condition of your flesh?

"Then Jesus said to his disciples, "If anyone would come after me, he must deny himself and take up his cross and follow me."
Matthew 16:24

"For we know that our old self was crucified with him so that the body of sin might be done away

with, that we should no longer be slaves to sin-because anyone who has died has been freed from sin."

Romans 6:6

"Those who belong to Christ Jesus have crucified the sinful nature with its passions and desires."
Galatians 5:24

THEY'RE BA-ACK!

It was March 3, 2022 and at 5am I was still in bed. Everything about this day is ingrained in my mind including the date. My everyday wake up time is between 7-7:30am and my husband is an early riser, even in retirement, between 5-6am and on some days 4am. That morning, I woke up to my husband shutting the bedroom doors, turning the hallway light on which shines in our bedroom and I heard the inside doors to the enclosed porch open. Again, I am a very light sleeper so all of the commotion woke me up. I could not understand why all the doors were being shut and opened and my first thought was, is my husband getting dementia and he does not know what he is doing. It was just odd!

I thought I better get up and play investigator in an unsuspecting way. Crawled out of bed, put my tennis shoes on, walked down the hallway and Earl (our cat) is at the end of the hallway meowing. That was odd that Earl was out of his night time room. I am the one that always lets Earl out in the morning and feeds him. It was just getting light outside and I walked in the dining room and could see the lights were on in the enclosed front porch and throughout the house. I also felt cool air coming from the enclosed front porch. I turned and looked for my husband in the living room and holy cow, it's a bat. I am pretty sure at that moment I did not say holy cow, because bats bring out the worst in me, along with snakes.

Chills hit my whole body and I ran to the back door and stood, in case the bat came flying my way, so I could open up the back door. For a moment I thought, maybe I should run out the back door and down the road and not come back. I knew right away why my husband was shutting all the doors to try and contain the bat to one room. I immediately asked him where the large fishing net was and he told me it was in the basement. He was able to get the bat contained to the living room and we stood at the French doors watching this flying mammal navigate the small area. At one point in time the bat kept hitting where the wall ends up by the ceiling. It looked like it was trying to get back up to the attic.

My husband decided to retrieve the fishing net and while he was doing that Earl came up to the French doors right next to me and looked in the living room. Earl started to bob his head up and down and back and forth, trying to keep up with the bats arial display. I am pretty sure Earl thought this was a bird and how fun it might be to be let in the living room for an opportunity to catch it. However, when the bat came close to the French doors flying low, Earl ducked his head down and took off running into the kitchen leaving me all by myself. My husband comes back into the dining room with the large fishing net, hat on, leather gloves to protect his hands and a hooded sweatshirt, with the hood up.

He walks out on the enclosed front porch and over to the other door that opens to the living room. He peeks his head around the door as if this is some giant that he has to capture and subdue. He steps into the living room and shuts the door behind him to the enclosed front porch. I have never seen my husband wave his arms so much and duck and weave. I thought he was more fascinating to watch than the bat. He kept telling me the bat looked like a blur flying by him. With that being said, I took it upon myself to give him directions after he swung the net and no bat went in. This was a big bat and also a mistake to give my husband directions!

It took about 10 minutes for him to catch the bat in the fishing net, even with my unwanted directions. With the bat contained, the topic of rabies came up again and should we get the bat tested for rabies. Our attempt over ten years ago to get the brain tested of a bat resulted in an inconclusive outcome because the brain had deteriorated too much. And why on earth would we get this one tested when we did not get the other 8 tested. Especially the one that was crawling under our bed and his or her buddy that was flying over our bed and sounded like it was having difficulty flying.

We decided not to get this one tested and IF it did have rabies than the decision comes whether to get rabies shots or not. All of a sudden, I could feel my post-traumatic stress bat disorder coming back. I walked down the hallway and heard something buzzing and immediately stopped and looked around and a stink bug flew by me and I started waving my arms. All morning my chills came and went and everywhere I walked in the house I looked up and around while I was walking. Even in the shower I kept looking up. Every little noise I heard, I stopped and looked around.

The day before was in the middle 60's and now it was back down to 32 degrees. For some reason the number of stink bugs had increased in the house overnight. Oh my gosh, this is March not June, July or August which is when bat season always was. We have not had a bat in our living quarters for about 10 years. How did this bat get into our living quarters? We

They're Ba-ack!

knew we still had bats in the attic, even with doing everything we knew how to do and what we had read to keep them out. We had found two dead ones in buckets in the attic after attempts to rid our house of them. This was so unsettling!

Looking back, there was only one time we had a bat by itself, all the other times we had two at once. Was there another one that was hiding and would come out in the middle of the night? Is this the only one for this year? Has the colony gotten so big we will have many more? The questions in my mind were endless. What if I took my oil and anointed all doors an went up in the attic and anointed the attic doors and crawled into where we know they might be and anoint that area, in the name of Jesus. Would that rid our house of EVERY critter that was still hiding and had not come out yet. My mind would not stop with the what ifs and all the unanswered questions.

How many times in our lives do we focus on the questions that we have no answers to? How about those would of, could of, should of, thoughts that we tend to dwell on? How about those whys that can throw us into a perpetual state of mind. The adversary is good at playing mind games and playing the same tapes in our minds over and over again. He wants us to focus on what will bring us down.

The questions we should ask are: Do I know for sure where I am going when I die? Do I go to church and just go through the motions? Do I act differently at church on Sunday and the rest of the week I am of the world? Do I praise and worship God? Do I have a prayer life? Do I want to be a servant of God or is it all about me?

"For God so loved the world that he gave his one and only Son, that whoever believes in him shall not perish but have eternal life."

John 3:16

"Do not conform any longer to the pattern of this world, but be transformed by the renewing of your mind. Then you will be able to test and approve what God's will is-his good, pleasing and perfect will."

Romans 12:2

Be joyful always; pray continually; give thanks in all circumstances, for this is God's will for you in Christ Jesus."

1 Thessalonians 5:16-17

"You my brothers, were called to be free. But do not use your freedom to indulge the sinful nature, rather, serve one another in love."

Galatians 5:13

STINK BUGS

The invasion of the stink bugs in the house has been part of our inside environment for several years. Stink bugs resemble a very small prehistoric looking bug, about ¼" wide and ½" long. Stink bugs snuck in from Asian countries. They seem to not have been blessed with the ability to fly well. Instead, they bumble around with an odd buzzing noise, flying into anything that gets in their path of flight. Sometimes hitting things, including me, and dropping to the floor. What's annoying about them is when captured or smashed they give out this foul odor. For me its indescribable.

I don't know how they get into the house but they make themselves at home, everywhere. I am assuming since we live in a house that was built in 1887, I have no doubt in my mind, they come in through all the cracks and crevice's. Just like the mice, snakes, and bats. Stink bugs like to hide in curtains, clothes, behind pictures, under cushions, you name it, they inhabit it. I have pulled slacks out of my closet and had stink bugs hanging on them. I was cleaning our laundry room, that has a breakfast nook in it, and upon removing the cushions, there were 20 stink bugs underneath. Don't know why I counted them. Sometimes I would get up in the morning and there will be dead stink bugs on the floor that were not there the night before. I have gone around picking up live ones, 4-5 in my hand and tossing them outside. They are everywhere, upstairs, main floor, basement, and enclosed front porch. It does not matter the outdoor temps; we have them year-round inside.

Spraying chemicals would not be good especially inside the house, so stink bugs as annoying as they are, have become a part of our lives. They all look alike and I have killed, thrown live ones outside, and picked up dead ones over the past several years. I would not be surprised if the count is in the thousands, with daily decluttering of the bugs at least 3-5 bugs per day. I don't believe they have a natural enemy, which allows them to reproduce quickly. Do I like the stink bugs, NO! Are they invasive, YES!

How many invasive things do we let into our lives that choke out our relationship with God? Just like the stink bugs, if I don't get rid of them on a daily basis, they will eventually take over the house and my time, energy and other more important things will be pushed aside. It's not easy spending time with God and reading the Bible. There are so many distractions in life today that can consume us. That's what the devil wants.

I used to tell God I would do it tomorrow and tomorrow would come and it would be the same thing. For me the thought of standing up God on a daily basis, even though he would give me grace and forgive me, was enough for me to make some changes. Jesus gave his life for us!

"but the worries of this life, the deceitfulness of wealth and the desires for other things come in and choke the word, making it unfruitful."
Mark 4:19

"Be self-controlled and alert. Your enemy the devil prowls around like a roaring lion looking for someone to devour."
1 Peter 5:8

One of my favorite verses!

"I can do everything through him who gives me strength."

Philippians 4:13

I can get rid of those invasive issues! In Jesus Name, Amen.

WORDS

It's pre spring as I call it, the first week of March. Temperatures are in the 40's for a couple of days. The weekend reaches 76 and five days later we are expecting 2-4" of snow. Winter can't seem to let go and spring has not sprung yet. It's always an exciting time when the buds start to appear on the forsythia and other spring time first bloomers. Even the birds that have over wintered are singing more. The buzzards came early this year! Blue jays, cardinals, red bellied wood peckers, robins, chickadees, just to name a few. We have not seen the blue birds yet and my husband and I always keep an eye out for them, trying to see who will be the one to catch a first glimpse.

They all have their own distinct song especially the black birds. Not sure I would call it a song but a loud mix of chatter. The black birds come in droves and like to hang out in our mature trees all over our yard. Usually, they land in two or three trees right next to each other and the chatter begins. Even when walking in the back yard, their chatter is so loud and when walking underneath the trees they have perched in, it can be almost deafening. Of course, we as humans have no idea what they are saying to each other and what each chirp, song and chatter means. Those black birds come back every year and their chatter never changes.

What is our chatter? Is it gossip? Is it negative and critical? Is it deceiving? Is it hurtful? Is it condemning? Is it all about us? Is it arrogant? Is it prideful? Our chatter should be encouraging, uplifting, thankful, supportive, compassionate, empathetic and full of love. Our chatter represents what's truly in our hearts! What's in your heart?

"But I tell you that men will have to give account on the day of judgment for every careless word they have spoken. For by your words you will be acquitted, and by your words you will be condemned."
Matthew 12:36-37

Words

"Do not let any unwholesome talk come out of your mouths, but only what is helpful for building others up according to their needs, that it may benefit those who listen."
Ephesians 4:29

"If anyone considers himself religious and yet does not keep a tight rein on his tongue, he deceives himself and his religion is worthless."
James 1:26

"The tongue has the power of life and death, and those who love it will eat its fruit."
Proverbs 18:21

HEART'S DESIRES

We all have dreams and goals and as we age and become closer to God, those dreams and goals change. One of my dreams is to have chickens which has been a dream of mine for 15 years. Living on 3.50 acres we have plenty of room for a brood of ladies. However, life gets in the way of our dreams and goals and we have to figure out with God's help what is and who is more important for certain seasons in our life. Being married and as us women do, we tend to sacrifice more of our dreams and goals for other people. In the big picture we are here to further God's kingdom not our kingdom. With that being said, I can still dream and pray and if it is in God's will, I will have chickens one day.

I have a vision of the chicken coop, one that looks like a church. The ladies would be my church ladies. I would have a sign saying, "bathing area," in which would be a mixture of dirt, sand, and ash for them to take dust baths. A plaque in the coop that reads, be a good egg and who knows what other novelties will adorn the inside and outside of the coop. The coop would be placed out by the garden, which would give the ladies another bath area and plenty of bugs and left-over veggies for an added treat to their diet. I would have a brood of 5 diverse ladies and their names would be Anastasia (resurrection), Yuna (gentle and kind hearted), Shaquana (truth in life) and sisters Audrey (noble strength) and Arvilla (eagle ruler).

I have been told never to name your chickens in case they end up on your dinner table, but how do you not name them, especially when their personalities start to come out. I am pretty sure mine would not end up on our dinner table. I have bought several used books on chicken raising and the do's and don'ts of raising a happy, healthy, and content brood. I have not given up on that dream!

What are your dreams and goals or heart's desires? Do we work hard at obtaining them or believe in our heart's that we are not worthy of having something? What are our reasons for trying to obtain certain things? Do our heart's desires match up with God's will for our lives? This year was the first year we came close to getting a coop and chickens, but that still small voice in me, which I believe is the Holy Spirit, said no. I don't know why but I have to obey and continue to believe that one day I will have my brood of chickens, even if it's in heaven. When I disconnect with the world and focus on God, that voice becomes very strong in me, and there is no doubt in what the answer is. God's timing is perfect!

"Delight yourself in the Lord and he will give you the desires of your heart."
Psalm 37:4

"May he give you the desires of your heart and make all your plans succeed."
Psalm 20:4

"The eyes of all look to you, and you give them their food at the proper time. You open your hand and satisfy the desires of every living thing."
Psalm 145:15-16

INTEGRITY

Married to an outdoorsman, I have come to accept the occasional live bait in the refrigerator. Sometimes we don't have a choice in matters. Went to grab my spring mix of greens out of the refrigerator and thought for sure I had finished them the day before. Not realizing my husband used the empty plastic container that I had put in the recycling bin, to fill with dirt and worms. Ugh! The challenge of finding your own bait, not only is cheaper but rewarding, whether digging for earth worms or small fish caught in a seine.

My husband uses a red head lamp at night, which worms can't see and therefore won't disappear back into the ground. So, on a misty, foggy evening in early spring, Mark heads out for the hunt and usually wants to have time to himself. However, Obie (our cat) is Marks buddy and Obie adores Mark. We have often said Obie behaves more like a dog than a cat. When Mark heads out, he specifically leaves Obie inside with me which does not settle well with Obie.

Obie starts by jumping up in our laundry room windows that sit about 5 feet off the ground. The washer and dryer make for an easier jump. He does not sit very long, hops down, runs through the house, and down the hall, sounding like two cats chasing each other but it's only one. Then into our bedroom jumping up on the window sill that sits maybe two feet from the floor. Again, does not sit very long, comes into the living room, looks at me and meows and goes back and repeats his antics until I give in and let him out.

Obie wants to be with Mark when he is outdoors. I looked out after a few minutes and in the glare of the red light pointing toward the ground, you could see Obie right around Mark's feet. Mark's first response when he opened the back door was, "Why did you let Obie out?" I told Mark, "Because Obie loves being with you and he kept running back and forth in the house from window to window, trying to keep track of you, and making a pit stop in the living room to holler at me." I was told never to let him out again during worm gathering.

My response was, "And why not, he loves being with you." Mark continued to tell me that Obie gets under his feet, it's dark out, and with Obie being black you can't see him well. Plus, when Mark finds a worm, Obie wants to be the first one to try and either bat at it with his paw or pick it up in his mouth. I told Mark, you have a helper. Mark told me he does not need a helper and I told him; I wish I had a helper that's as dependent as Obie is and you can count on him during every worm hunt.

Can your family and friends count on you? Do you do what you say you are going to do? Have you committed to help someone, but something better comes up and you cancel? Can people trust you with your words? How is your moral compass?

"The integrity of the upright guides them, but the unfaithful are destroyed by their duplicity."
Proverbs 11:3

"The Lord detests lying lips, but he delights in men who are truthful."
Proverbs 12:22

"Do to others as you would have them do to you."
Luke 6:31

HELL

It's October and about the time to start the wood burner to take the chill out of the house. We have no insulation in the walls, which are three brick wide or 16" wide including the plaster. It can be 60-70 degrees outside with 40-50 degrees at night and the house stays usually at around 60 degrees, which is what we keep the thermostat on in winter. Long johns are our winter apparel and sometimes my Carhartt winter pullover hat is my morning apparel. I am wadding up the newspaper and laying it in the wood burner on the grate, then I put some kindling on it and several small slender pieces about 20" long.

Having a wood burner for 16 years and being the head fire starter and the keeper of the wood burner, I have learned to start a fire quickly, by opening the bottom ash door to let more air in. I bent down, struck a match, lit the newspaper and reached down to open the ash door to let some air in and off the fire took. All of a sudden, I hear chirping. This can't be happening again, another bird in the stove pipe. I almost started to panic and knew the bird was feeling the heat and smoke.

There was no way I could put out the fire quickly. You definitely don't put water in a wood burner. I shut the ash door as soon as I heard chirping and the only option I had was to close the air off to the fire, which would eventually choke it out, but not quick enough to save the bird. The bird started chirping louder and there was no pause between chirps. I knew what was happening and I had to leave the room with my hands over my ears. I stayed in the laundry room which is in the back of the house for several minutes. Coming back in the living room, there was silence. The fire was dying down with no air and I knew the bird was dead.

By the time my husband got home, the fire was out. I explained to him what had happened and if he could remove the bird and figure out why the birds are coming down the stove pipe. The bird was removed first and it was another starling. My husband put a screen in the cap which was on top of the outside stove pipe. He accomplished that within a couple of days. As I was plugging my ears and leaving the room, I thought about hell and what that must be like.

The Bible talks about a heaven and a hell and that we can either choose life or death. God gives everyone of us free will to choose. Along with Satan and for those who reject Christ, their final destination is the lake of fire (hell).

"And I saw the dead, great and small, standing before the throne, and books were opened. Another book was opened, which is the book of life. The dead were judged according to what they had done as recorded in the books. The sea gave up the dead that were in it and death and Hades gave up the dead that were in them and each person was judged according to what he had done. Then death and Hades were thrown into the lake of fire. The lake of fire is the second death. If anyone's name was not found written in the book of life, he was thrown into the lake of fire."

Revelations 20:12-15

The Bible talks in parables and Matthew 13:36-43 explains that at the end of the world the good will be separated from the bad and the bad, *"They will throw them into the fiery furnace, where there will be weeping and gnashing of teeth. Then the righteous will shine like the sun in the Kingdom of their Father. He who has ears. Let him hear." (Matthew 13:42-43)*

The last part of this scripture, "He who has ears. Let him hear." Do we really hear this scripture? We don't have a description of hell other than a fiery furnace and weeping and gnashing of teeth. We all know what a fiery furnace is like, HOT. Will there be a constant smell of sulfur for eternity? Will you be so hot that your thirst will never be quenched because there is no water in a fiery furnace? What will happen to your skin? Will people be screaming and begging to get out? Will people be cursing at God? Will people have regrets because they did not listen or hear the ones that tried to tell them the truth? My description of hell is torment for eternity. All I know is I don't want to go to hell.

NAUGHTY LIST

Here we go again! I say that because I don't want to use an expletive. Many moons ago I drove a straight truck and graduated to a semi and when I came off of the road, I was a dispatcher. When you hang around certain people you become those people if you are not careful. As much as I hate to admit it, I had a potty mouth. God has done a work in my mouth after much repentance and prayer. However, I am still a work in progress.

My husband comes in one evening at dark, mid-summer and tells me Obie chased a grown kitten up a tree by our back door. I asked him what a grown kitten means and he did not know. My thinking is, 6–12 months-old. The next day Obie and Earl wanted outside and Earl stayed in the barn for most of the day, which is unusual. Especially because he missed his lunch. I walked out to the barn to look around and Earl was sitting in the barn looking around and all of a sudden, I see this little black flash run by me. It was definitely not a grown kitten, it was a small kitten. UGH! I called it in a high pitched but soft voice, you know the usual kitty, kitty, kitty and I received a very soft but hoarse meow back. It was scared and very leery of me and it would not let me get close.

I gathered my thoughts and having the God given gift of mercy, I could not let this little kitten stay outside any longer. I returned to the house and gathered up one of the carry kennels, a bowl of the boy's special urinary cat food, a pair of gloves, and a long sleeve shirt to protect my arms. After about 2-3 hours, this poor little kitten, so tired and hungry, wanted to sleep, which gave me several opportunities to get closer.

My gloves were on and I had the opportunity to grab it as soon as it closed its eyes and dropped its head. Glad I had my gloves on! Got it in the carry kennel and took it inside on our enclosed front porch. We had a little female, 5-6 weeks old and what is called a tuxedo cat. She looks like she has a tuxedo on, white fur that starts in between her eyes, runs down her nose and goes down her chest and all the way down her underneath, with four white paws. My husband tells her she is overdressed all the time.

After several vet appointments and an attempt to a new residence that did not work out, Lilly came back to live with us. As her personality and antics came out, it had become very apparent that she was a little destructive. I don't think intentionally but out of curiosity and as kittens/cats do, they like to climb and the higher the better. A resin 3ft high candle holder was broken into three pieces. A resin 4ft tall pillar that had a fake plant on it was broken into three pieces. Two buffet lamps knocked over and broken. The two lamps had stink bugs on the inside of the shades, so I guess I could blame the stink bugs. My clothes that hung close to the ground, pants and long dresses had pulls in them. I started having to kitten proof the house.

However, a full-grown Lilly is still wreaking havoc at times. Heard a big bang in the middle of the night and flew out of bed. The fire extinguisher in the living room had been knocked over. Did not go looking further and when I got up in the morning, Mark told me I should go look in the dining room. Oh my gosh! I can't even go there. With each incident I would call out her name and tell her she was on the naughty list and that she was going to have a hard time getting off of it if she did not stop her behavior. I don't think I will be decorating for the holidays for several years.

Have you ever been on the naughty list? Have you never gotten off of the naughty list? Are you an obedient or disobedient Christian? Do you hang around people who are constantly on the naughty list? People who sow discord, who love drama, arguments, fights, gossip, steal because they feel entitled. Someone who is constantly sinning, but feels because of God's grace they are forgiven each time and can continue their behavior. The list can go on and on. As Christians we have to check ourselves and check the people we associate with.

In *Romans 8:5-8* Paul talks about 2 different kinds of people, those that follow the spirit (God) and those that follow the flesh. *"Those who live according to the sinful nature have their minds set on what that nature desires; but those who live in accordance with the Spirit have their minds set on what the Spirit desires. The mind of sinful man is death, but the mind controlled by the Spirit is life and peace; the sinful mind is hostile to God. It does not submit to God's law, nor can it do so. Those controlled by the sinful nature cannot please God."*

"A scoundrel and villain, who goes about with a corrupt mouth, who winks with his eye, signals with his feet and motions with his fingers, who plots evil with deceit in his heart-he always stirs up dissension. Therefore disaster will overtake him in an instant; he will suddenly be destroyed-without remedy. There are six things the Lord hates, seven that are detestable to him: haughty eyes, a lying tongue, hands that shed innocent blood, a heart that devises wicked schemes, feet that are quick to rush into evil, a false witness who pours out lies and a man who stirs up dissension among brothers."
Proverbs 6:12-19

"The Lord detests lying lips, but he delights in men who are truthful."
Proverbs 12:22

"The Lord detests the thoughts of the wicked, but those of the pure are pleasing to him."
Proverbs 15:26

TEMPTATION

I have two sisters and I am the middle one. I can always remember our visits to Grandma K's house in Broad Ripple, IN. The Thanksgivings, where the girl cousins spent the night and made name tags and other Thanksgiving table décor. Grandma's oyster dressing, Smuckers black raspberry jam, apple salad, macaroni and cheese, and just being around grandma, are such good memories! On a visit to grandma's one summer with our parents, grandma called us to the back door. She grabbed a handful of peanuts, looked at us girls and said in a stern voice, "Don't ever try this."

She opened the back door and low and behold a squirrel was waiting outside the door. She laid the peanuts on the open palm of her hand and stuck it out close to the top step. All of a sudden, this squirrel came up to her hand with no hesitation and took the peanuts and left. Wow! Of course, as little girls we thought that was great and look what grandma could do! How fun! Again, grandma looked at us and said in a stern voice, "Don't ever try this." As we all walked back into the house toward the living room, us girls kept talking about the squirrel and how it came up to grandma and took the peanuts and how cute the squirrel was. The adults were talking and mom looked around and asked where my younger sister was. We did not know. Mom got up and headed toward the back door and my younger sister who was 5 at the time was crying and holding her hand. Uh oh! Grandma came to the door and asked her if she had tried to feed the squirrel. Of course, that was my younger sister. God love her!

After inspecting her hand and finding a little mark, hands were washed, and the Dr. was called. As hands were being washed and my sister was being questioned, we found out she used a Keebler Pin Stripe cookie that grandma always had, either in the clown cookie jar or in a package on the kitchen table. Word got around the neighborhood that Arvilla's granddaughter was bitten by a squirrel. Several of the men in the neighborhood decided they were going to find the squirrel and shoot it. What? I will never forget that day and it is still in my mind so clear as if it was just yesterday.

We were told to stay in the house and let the men find the squirrel. A couple of the men had shot guns and they were looking up in the trees walking around the neighborhood. I asked my mom how are they going to know which squirrel it was. I thought that was an appropriate question. As on many occasions I was told to hush. No squirrels were shot and when everything calmed down, we left grandmas. Squirrels rarely get rabies but the Dr. told my parents she needed to get rabies shots. I don't remember the number of shots she received. I do remember thinking how brave she was to go through that, along with the lectures she got from grandma and mom and dad.

We all deal with temptations and the consequences that come with them. We know we shouldn't do something but we do it anyway. Being a Christian is a lifelong journey to become Christ like. Being saved gives us the Holy Spirit that lives inside of us so that we can have the power to sin less as we grow in our Christian walk. For me memorizing Bible scripture works for temptations and knowing who God is.

"I do not understand what I do. For what I want to do I do not do, but what I hate I do."
                              Romans 7:15

"On reaching the place, he said to them, "Pray that you will not fall into temptation."
                              Luke 22:40

"And lead us not into temptation, but deliver us from the evil one."
                              Matthew 6:13

THIRST

We had a knock at the door one Saturday morning when we lived in the city. Answering the door, I found a boy about the age of 7-8, selling candy for his school. His mother was standing on the walkway and he looked at me and told me we had two kittens living under our porch. What? We had an opening on both sides of our concrete porch and sure enough two kittens come running out. After buying a chocolate bar, he and his mother were on their way to the next house. My husband was standing behind me and as they left, we both stepped out on the porch and here are two kittens. My husband to this day swears that mother and her little boy put those kittens under our porch to get rid of them.

At the time I told him they seemed too nice to do something like that. Although, with all of the stray cats we have had, I don't put it past anyone. We already had two neutered males, one my husband got when he was a kitten (Lambert) and Jake was a stray. I knew we could not handle four cats, so at that time you were able to take an animal to the Humane Society, unlike today. We kept the female and took her brother in. She ruled the roost until we got a Brittany and for some reason, he left the boys alone but wanted to chase her. She lived in our upstairs for a couple of years and would not come down.

By the time we moved to a rural area and into an old farmhouse, Jake and Lambert had died. Was not sure how she would handle the new house but on arrival she got out of her carry kennel and decided she was not going to be contained anymore to an upstairs. Abby became very comfortable very quickly to the main level and for some reason Morgan our Brittany decided to leave her alone. Go figure that one out. Abby started to drink an enormous amount of water and she could not seem to quench her thirst and her eating slowed down. An examination from the veterinarian and blood work showed she was diabetic. I had no idea cats could get diabetes. Because her levels were so high the vet suggested she be on insulin. Insulin?

How much is that going to cost and for how long? With any animal medical diagnosis there is always the decision, do we proceed, do we stop treatment, it's just an animal. How much do we spend, etc. Our pets become part of the family and for some their kids, as silly as that sounds. After much thought we started her on insulin with one shot per day, however, she became insulin resistant. Abby continued to decline and her thirst could not be satisfied. She drank and drank and drank and drank and I was always filling up her water bowls. After a couple of years on insulin, becoming insulin resistant, not wanting to eat much, and the inevitable not wanting to use the litter box or not being able to make it to the litter box. I made the difficult decision to have her put down. My fondest memory of her was she always slept next to my pillow at night and never got up in the morning until I got up.

Do you have a thirst that can't be satisfied? Are you searching for something to fill that emptiness? Are you unsatisfied in life but you have no idea how to fix it? Does your soul constantly desire something?

I encourage you to read *John 4* which is the story of the woman at the well. Jesus told her when a person drinks the water from the well, they *"will be thirsty again."* Those who drink the water that Jesus gives them *"will never thirst."* This water is spiritual water to nourish the soul and give eternal life. I encourage you to take a drink! You won't regret it!

"On the last and greatest day of the Feast, Jesus stood and said in a loud voice, "If anyone is thirsty, let him come to me and drink. Whoever believes in me, as the Scripture has said, streams of living water will flow from within him."
John 7:37-38

"Jesus answered, "Everyone who drinks this water will be thirsty again, but whoever drinks the water I give him will never thirst. Indeed, the water I give him will become in him a spring of water welling up to eternal life."
John 4:13-14

"Blessed are those who hunger and thirst for righteousness, for they will be filled."
Matthew 5:6

PARENTS

We had the privilege one summer of having a den of foxes about 200 feet from our back door, in the old hollow oak tree that was in our open field. We had no idea mom, dad, and their kits were going to be a part of our summer. In my usual scanning of the back yard before opening the door, I saw what I thought was a small dog sitting on the large pile of dirt in front of the oak tree. The pile of dirt is about 4 feet tall by about 8 feet wide and came out of our house crawl space. I kept looking toward the oak tree and I thought I saw another dog sitting next to the one I saw first. Oh great, stray dogs. That's all we need.

I grabbed the binoculars that we keep by the back door and low and behold there were two foxes, one smaller and one bigger. Throughout the day I kept watch off and on and realized they might have a den in the old oak tree. I had been out working in the garden which was only 10 feet from the pile of dirt. I had been cutting the grass around the oak tree and I saw nothing to indicate we had any animals living in and under the oak tree. Nothing! The term "sly as a fox" comes to mind. That mama and papa fox sure pulled one over on us.

We spent the summer watching mama and papa take care of the five kits as they were growing up. Mama and papa were excellent parents and one was always on guard watching their surroundings while the kits were playing and the other parent was hunting for food for the family. On one occasion mama was sitting on top of another pile of dirt that is part of our shooting range. She was watching the 25-acre field behind us and the kits were running around chasing and jumping over each other. All of a sudden, the play stopped and mama changed her position on the pile of dirt from sitting to standing. Not sure if she vocalized something to the kits or just her demeaner showed that they knew something was coming.

Two of the kits ran up on the pile of dirt and stood with mama and the other three stopped and looked toward the field. I saw something coming and thought for sure it was a coyote. Oh my! All six of them were motionless and without hesitation one of the kits took off after what I thought was a coyote, turned out to be papa. The reason I know it was papa, he was much bigger than mama. The excitement that kit displayed was so heartwarming. One other kit ran up to papa who had brought them something to eat. Two of the five went back to playing and mama took over as soon as papa dropped the food. He did not stay long. I felt like I spent the majority of my summer watching these two parents raise their young.

Toward the end of the summer, I looked out back and saw mama and only one kit. They were both sitting on top of the dirt pile. We have no idea what happened to the other 4, although I think in our heart, we knew but did not want to talk about it. After that day we never saw mama or papa or any kits again. With each year I was hoping mama or another fox would make another den in the same oak tree, however, the skunks took it over.

We all have parents and some sacrifice their lives for their children to make sure their kids have everything they did not have. Good or bad? Some parents can be nurturing, controlling, out to lunch emotionally, selfish, drug addicts, alcoholics, abusive mentally, and physically, etc. Parents do their best with what they were given and some parents weren't given much from their parents. Sometimes it leaves open wounds and scars in our lives.

What if I told you there is a parent/father who can heal those wounds. What if I told you I knew a parent/father who loves you unconditionally. Who forgives you for your past mess ups, present mess ups, and future mess ups. A father who will never leave you. A father who knows what is best for you and who can provide a life you never dreamed you could have. A father who will meet all your needs. A father who always keeps His promises. A father who corrects you without being condescending. A father who is compassionate, full of grace and abounding in mercy and love. It's our Heavenly Father!

"How great is the love the Father has lavished on us, that we should be called children of God! And that is what we are!"

1 John 3:1

"Yet, O Lord, you are our Father. We are the clay, you are the potter, we are all the work you your hand."

Isaiah 64:8

This is the Lord's prayer I grew up with.

"Our Father, who art in heaven, hallowed be thy name; thy kingdom come, thy will be done, on earth as it is in heaven. Give us this day our daily bread. And forgive us our trespasses, as we forgive those who trespass against us. And lead us not into temptation, but deliver us from evil. For thine is the kingdom, the power and the glory, forever. Amen[i]

"The Lord himself goes before you and will be with you: he will never leave you nor forsake you. Do not be afraid; do not be discouraged."
                              Deuteronomy 31:8

CHOOSE YOUR BATTLES

Morgan had the misfortune of breaking one of his toes in four places on his left hind leg. We had no idea how he broke it, he just started limping. I was told it was a non-weight bearing toe and that if it did not heal it could be removed or the bones could be pinned together, which is not what I wanted to hear. The vet started the arduous task of splinting his paw and thought it would be better if he took Morgan in the back room to do this. Upon Morgan's arrival back in the examining room I noticed the splint came half way up his leg. I was told it would be on for four to six weeks and that they saw no problem with the toe healing provided we could keep the toe in the right position.

I already knew this was not going to be an easy task because of his high energy level and of course the vet had to remind me, because of his breed, it was not going to be easy to keep him contained and quite for six weeks. I was given instructions and a prescription to help calm him when needed and we were on our way. Knowing the next six weeks were going to be a challenge, as soon as we were in the car, I looked over at Morgan and said, "Let's go get some comfort food." So, we headed across the street to Burger King. I ordered my usual Whopper with cheese and fries and ordered Morgan a hamburger.

I did not give Morgan people food on a regular basis and that was the first time I had ever stopped to order something for him. For some reason I felt we both deserved some comfort food knowing what lay ahead of us and knowing what Morgan just had to go through. As soon as we got home Morgan inhaled the burger with no bun and I enjoyed one of my favorite fast-food meals.

We tried our best over the next several weeks and even with the help of medication to keep him calm. Morgan ended up cracking the hard plastic splint after about three weeks and we had to have a new one put on. Morgan had annual checkups at this vet and we had boarded him numerous times with them. For some reason they couldn't seem to get his gender correct and continued to call him a her, even after many corrections from mom. I know the name Morgan can be a boy or girls name, but come on, it is in his chart.

Upon completion of the new splint, they brought him into the waiting room with pink tape that covered the splint and reminded me how important it was to keep him contained and calm. PINK TAPE! My first thought was, but he is a boy not a girl. Being the non-confrontational person that I am and afraid they would think I was making too big of a deal out of the situation, I said nothing. As I stood there waiting to be checked out, I knew they had other colors that could have been used because the first splint definitely did not have pink tape on it.

A lady came in with her dog and as we were both waiting in line she came right up to Morgan and started commenting on the pink tape. I was not going to let someone else assume Morgan was a girl and I interrupted and said, "Yea, they think he is a girl." She looked at Morgan and told him she thought he was probably real comfortable with himself and that the pink tape would not bother him. I kept telling myself, Mary he is just a dog. But as us pet owners know our pets become a part of the family and for some, our children.

By the end of the week that pink tape was starting to discolor, even though we covered the splint every time we let Morgan out and by the end of the six weeks you could not tell it was pink. I realized I should have been grateful that a splint was put on and in the big picture the color did not matter, what mattered was that it healed. Morgan's toe healed at the end of the six-week period and not only was I elated that the splint had been taken off but he seemed so much more relaxed that it was gone.

In our own lives, how many times do we choose the wrong battles and react before we think or even react before we talk to God? We have to choose what is God's desires and not our own. We have to learn to let go of the small things and find something to be grateful for in the situation. As the saying goes, "don't sweat the small stuff."

"Do everything without complaining or arguing."
Philippians 2:14-15

"But I tell you that men will have to give account on the day of judgement for every careless word they have spoken."
Matthew 12:36

"...give thanks in all circumstances, for this is God's will for you in Christ Jesus."
1 Thessalonians 5:18

SNAKES

My husband warned me several times that we would have a snake or snakes that would come into our home. I tried to put that thought on the back burner but knew at some point in time that would be brought to the front burner. We knew a couple who lived in an 1800's brick farm house and they ended up having one under their stove. I knew it was coming, but did not know the time or place. Usually in spring and summer I would see the occasional garter snake and Obie our cat liked to catch small garter snakes around 6-8 inches and bring them to you. I also had seen a snake hanging in a hole inside one of our large dead ash trees and looked it up in one of our "Ohio Reptile" books and identified it as a milk snake.

That was outside and could somewhat deal with them on an outdoor basis. My husband was in the basement one day and hollered for me to come to the basement door. I thought he might need some help as I had become the flashlight holder, get me this, can you hold this, person. I was in the process of doing something and hollered back, "Just a minute, let me finish this and I will be right there." As I was turning to walk down our long hallway to get to the basement door, my husband had already opened the basement door and was starting to come down the hallway toward me. As I looked at him, I saw a snake that he was holding and it had wrapped itself around his arm.

Oh my gosh, the day had finally come! I did not know squealing noises could come out of me and I stopped dead in my tracks. My husband looked at me and said, "You can come closer." What was he thinking? Why would I want to do that? He told me he had a good hold on the snake and I was going to be ok to come closer. Oh, what the heck, I might as well try and get use to this because something tells me this was not going to be the last snake we would encounter in the house. It did not look like a garter snake and looked like a milk snake that I had seen outdoors. Milk snakes are nonpoisonous constrictors.

My husband proceeded to tell me it was in the crawl space and he just happened to look over at the crawl space entrance and it was watching him. We have a partial basement under about half of the house and the rest is crawlspace. My husband took the snake outdoors and let it loose. I guess as long as they stay in the basement/crawlspace that's ok. From that day forward every time my husband was in the basement and called for me, I always asked him if he had a snake.

About 5 years later during the summer, Mark was in the basement and I was outdoors on our zero-turn mowing. All of a sudden, I looked up and saw Mark coming toward me with one hand waving. Knowing he wanted something, I slowed down and came to a stop. I noticed another snake wrapped around his arm and here comes the squealing sounds out of me. The closer he got I kept thinking, please don't tell me this one was in the house. I shut the mower off so we could hear each other and he told me it was another crawl space snake.

I hate snakes and will never get use to this! Snakes give me the creepy crawlies, send chills and goose bumps all over me with an uneasy feeling for hours after seeing one. At times I have felt like I could lose my breakfast/lunch. That's the effect they have on me. Ok, that was the second one and as long as we have one on occasion, I need to get over it. I need to put my big girl panties on and deal with it. Fast forward two years. I needed to go upstairs and open the windows to let some fresh air in. We only used our finished upstairs as storage, so we did not go up very often, usually only to open the windows and close them before a rain. Oh, and to set mouse traps in the attic.

It was a hot summer day and I knew it would be stifling upstairs. As I approached the landing at the top of the stairs, I turned right into what would have been a bedroom. That was the only room that had carpet in it, the rest of the upstairs were the original wood floors. We had boxes and other items laying around, so to get to the window in that room I had to walk around a few things. When I was about two feet from the window, I came upon a snake. Oh my gosh! I let out a loud squeal and froze. I was surprised the snake did not move and thought because it was so hot upstairs it was probably a little lethargic.

I kept squealing and started to back up very slowly and continued to back up until I got to the steps and turned and went back downstairs, squealing all the way down. I wanted to run down the stairs but with a fused ankle and fused partial foot, that was impossible. After finding my cell phone and calling my husband, like he could do something being at work. He told me to just leave it and he would get it when he got home. Leave it, what if it goes somewhere and we don't know where it went, easy for him to say. Just like the bats! I knew since I was not going to attempt to pick it up, I had no choice, but to leave it.

I hung up the phone and immediately said in a loud voice, "Lord, what are we doing?" This Bible scripture came to mind, *"I can do everything through him who gives me strength." (Philippians 4:13).* I decided I was going back up and put a five-gallon bucket over the snake and keep it contained until my sweetheart got home. If God is on my side there is nothing I can't do, right? Found a five-gallon bucket in our tool room and made the creepy crawly journey back upstairs. I could feel the goose bumps and chills as I was going up the stairs, but kept repeating that scripture out loud and in my mind. As soon as I saw the snake, I started the snake squealing.

I was not sure it would still be there, but got close and sure enough it was still in the same position. With bucket in hand and still squealing, I put the bucket over the snake and it still did not move. With the snake contained I opened the windows and while slowly walking and looking around, went into the other room and opened those windows. On my way downstairs I started thanking God for what I was able to do. As soon as Mark arrived from work, we both went upstairs. I stood at a distance while Mark took the five gallon bucket off. He looked down and turned to me and said, "It is dead and has been dead for a while." What! That is why it never moved when I got close.

I did not know whether to cry, hang my head in shame and go back down stairs, start laughing, role my eyes, or just be quiet. I shook my head and just stayed quiet. We assumed it slithered through the walls and came through the small open areas where the boiler pipes went into the floors. Mark thought it probably could not figure out how to get back out and with it being so hot upstairs and with no food, it could not survive. We were pretty sure this was another milk snake. Will there be more? Not sure, but what I do know God will give me what I need to get through the next one, even if I do squeal a little.

Things come up in life that we think are impossible to do. But scripture tells us we can do everything and we can draw on God for strength and courage. It does not say that we will be only able to do certain things in life, it says EVERYTHING!

"I can do everything through him who gives me strength."

Philippians 4:13

"…Be strong and courageous, and do the work. Do not be afraid or discouraged, for the Lord God, my God is with you…"
   1 Chronicles 28:20

"Be strong and courageous. Do not be afraid or terrified because of them, for the Lord your God goes with you; he will never leave you nor forsake you."
   Deuteronomy 31:6-8

FRUIT OF THE SPIRIT

Living in a rural area brings with it much unwanted stray cats and the occasional stray dog. I woke up one hot summer morning to a faint meow that sounded so helpless. I lay in bed watching the windows and a very small kitten jumped up on the window ledge that's only maybe 12" from the ground. My heart goes out to unwanted, stray, hurting animals that are helpless in so many situations. I got out of bed, quickly, got dressed, and went outside to hopefully capture the little one before our dog was let out of his kennel. Upon approaching the very small kitten, it took off, forgetting there was a window well underneath. It hit the window well and darted off around the front of the house into some bushes. I slowly followed behind and when I reached the bushes, I crouched down talking to it in a very calm but gentle voice.

Poor thing, it was not going to let me near it. Every time I got to close for its comfort, it would hiss at me. Thought it best I leave it alone and went back out later. I have no idea where it came from, I am assuming someone dumped it. There were no other kittens around. After a coffee break, I thought out where I was going to put the kitten when I brought it into the house. I knew from our dog's behavior when seeing stray cat's way out in the field, if I did not protect this kitten, it would not end up well.

I put our large dog carry kennel on the front enclosed porch, with a small litter box and blanket inside the carrier. After much patience and two hours of sitting and talking to it, I had moved close enough to grab it, held on tight, and got to the house as soon as possible. For those of you who have cats and have to give them medicine, pill or liquid form, it's like going into combat. You can come out of that experience scratched, frazzled, bit, cat hair all over you and your surroundings. You can have a real since of accomplishment, if the medicine goes down the throat, even with battle scars.

Not sure what this little kitten had been through before it arrived at our house, but it seemed like it might have been traumatic. Probably should have grabbed it by the scruff of the neck to prevent my scratches, however, when grabbing a stray kitten, it's however you can grab it. Over the next several weeks until I could acclimate Morgan (dog), when going on the porch the kitten would back up in the carrier and hiss. I got it to the vet, we had a male, maybe seven weeks old, underweight and one feisty kitten. All of the strays that come to our house get fixed, that is the rule when you show up at our house.

I started feeding it three small meals, three times a day to get some weight on him. We had not planned on keeping him but after being on a list at the local Humane Society and not hearing from anyone for months, he became a part of our family. Now, we needed a name. The joke around our family is because we live in London, OH, the queen lives in London and I am the queen. When talking to my younger sister about naming this kitten she said, "Since you are the queen, what about some of the different queen's son's names?"

Like, Edward, Prince Leopold, (Duke of Albany), Alfred, Prince Arthur, just to name a few. After much thinking and looking up the rankings of Duke or Earl, Earl would not leave my mind. Even though it was a ranking in the royal families, the more his personality came out, we had a name, Earl. The first time we took him to the vet to board him, upon pick up day the vet assistant brought Earl out and looked at me and said, "Earl fits him perfectly." Yes! Pretty sure she did not mean he acted like royalty. Since I fed Earl three times a day when he was little, to this day at the age of 15, he demands he still gets fed three times a day. Breakfast is whenever mom gets up much to Earl's dismay and he manages to come out to the kitchen at noon and 5pm. We have to separate both males at night so Earl has his own room, his own bed, food bowl, water bowl, and two litter boxes.

Earl is very particular about his litter boxes and I learned that it was better to have two for him. Earl likes to be touched only at his choosing. Earl does not like to be picked up at all and will fight you tooth and nail to get out of the comforting and gentle hold of mom and dad. My husband and I have become Earl's staff. After writing all of this so far, I am thinking Earl acts like royalty. When we do not get up in the morning when Earl thinks we should, he starts howling.

Believe it or not his howling sounds like someone is saying, hellooooo. The first time I heard this coming out of a sleep, I thought for sure someone had entered our home. Before going any further, I lay there and listened and could not believe what I was hearing. Hellooooo, Hellooooo. Our little boy can talk! If Earl hears you move in bed, he changes octaves and it becomes a higher pitch and he continues and continues and continues until you get up and feed him. Earl likes to dawdle at the back door and upon wanting out, stands there and smells the air, scans the backyard and might decide to go out or stay in.

We love Earl, but sometimes all of his attitudes and behaviors can be a little daunting and difficult to be around. Do we have attitudes and behaviors in our lives that are not so desirable? Do we have anger, bitterness, hate, selfishness? Are we impatient, cranky, stubborn, defiant, unhappy, negative, critical, or just all around miserable? Or are we striving for the fruits of the spirit which are love, patience, joy, kindness, peace, goodness, faithfulness, gentleness, and self-control. I don't know about you but I want every goodness that God has for me and want to stand out in a delightful way. I want people to know there is something different about me.

"But the fruit of the Spirit is love, joy, peace, patience, kindness, goodness, faithfulness, gentleness, and self-control..."
Galatians 5:22-23

"Love is patient, love is kind. It does not envy, it does not boast, it is not proud. It is not rude, it is not self-seeking, it is not easily angered, it keeps no record of wrongs. Love does not delight in evil but

rejoices with the truth. It always protects, always trusts, always hopes, always perseveres."
1 Corinthians 13:4-7

"Be completely humble and gentle; be patient, bearing with one another in love."
Ephesians 4:2

INVITATION

I hope you have enjoyed reading my stories as much as I enjoyed writing them. I don't believe this book would have ever come to being written if it wasn't for my husband, salvation and the nudging of the Holy Spirit. I want to give you the opportunity to make Jesus the Lord of your Life. Years ago, what I called Bible Beaters, you know, those people that want you to come to church. Those people that want to quote Bible scripture all the time. Those people that ask you if you know where you are going when you die. Those people who you see coming and avoid them at all cost. You know them!

The ones that want to beat you over the head with their Bibles, until you get it. Maybe some of their approaches are not correct and maybe some of them refuse to meet you where you were at. Maybe some of them seem so high and mighty and when you look at their lives, they are no different than you or me. Maybe some of them just sincerely care. Whatever the reasons are that we want to evade them, those Bible Beaters had something I needed. I always thought I had to be religious to know God and no one ever told me it was a personal relationship with God that matures over time. I asked God to come into my heart in the early 80's and read the Bible off and on and went to church off and on.

I would have called myself a non-practicing Christian. Suffering from depression, lame attempt at suicide, then all hell broke loose and something tragic happened to my ankle that changed my life drastically. I was struggling to get through each day. Six, foot/ankle surgeries over a 20-year period, dependence on prescribed narcotics, drug withdrawals, and depression hit again and life was overwhelming. I finally turned to God and He was patient enough to wait! I started reading the Bible, watching as much Christian television as possible, listening to praise and worship songs and praying.

I learned to accept the fact that life was going to change for me. I had to find a new normal. I learned how to deal with chronic foot pain that at times over took my days. I learned that God was there for me 24/7 and when people were not there for me, God always was. *"The Lord himself goes before you and will be with you; he will never leave you nor forsake you." (Deuteronomy 31:8).* I learned that God was a healing God and that I could defeat my depression, but it took work on my part.

I learned that life not always turns out the way we think it should and that life is not fair at times, but that God takes our trials and disappointments and can turn them around for good, if we allow Him to. *"And we know that in all things God works for the good of those who love him, who have been called according to his purpose." (Romans 8:28).* I learned that God gives us promises in the Bible and he ALWAYS keeps his promises. I learned the Bible is full of God's principles and if we follow God's principles, life becomes full of God's blessings. I learned that I could have joy and gratefulness in the midst of difficult trials. I learned I could have joy even with 23 years of chronic foot pain!

I could go on and on and share with you all that God has done for me, things that I never imagined and it's because I have a personal relationship with him. I want to give you the opportunity to have what I have and to have someone very special in your life who loves you unconditionally. Please take this time to say this salvation prayer, it's a free gift and it's so simple. With faith, pray:

Lord Jesus, I know that I am a sinner and I ask for your forgiveness. I believe you died for my sins and rose from the dead. I turn from my sins and invite you into my heart and life. I want to trust and follow you as my Lord and savior. In Jesus name, Amen.

If you prayed this pray, I am ecstatic for you!

ABOUT THE AUTHOR

Over 20 years ago Mary suffered a traumatic injury to her ankle. After six surgeries and lots of recovery time on her hands, a new normal had to be found, so she started writing stories. Through her faith, she had the desire to share the lessons she learned from nature. Mary's husband of 38 years introduced her to his love of hunting and fishing. The numerous deer, squirrel, and hunting trips gave her such an appreciation of God's handiwork and the lessons we can learn from not only nature's beauty, but from all the animals that we share with the earth. Although her ankle injury now prevents her from hunting and fishing, natures lessons continue at her country home in other forms, whether it's bats in the attic, a bird that found its way down the stove pipe, and many more. It has been exciting, scary, and rewarding for these critters to enter into Mary and her husband's lives for more lessons.

Mary is a native of Indianapolis and moved to Columbus, Ohio after meeting her husband. Mary loves to use humor not only in her writings but in everyday life situations. As she says, "It lightens the load." Rural Indiana is their home now. Mary enjoys being part of a prison ministry and when the opportunity arises, she shares her battle with depression and how God as taken her from darkness to light.

ENDNOTES

---

[i] Memorized as a child, taken from The Book of Common Prayer. Matthew 6:9-13

New International Version
All scripture taken from the Holy Bible, New International Version ®. Copyright © 1973, 1978, 1984 by International Bible Society. Used by permission of Zondervan. All rights reserved.

www.ingramcontent.com/pod-product-compliance
Lightning Source LLC
LaVergne TN
LVHW051051080426
835508LV00019B/1815